11+

Vocabulary

Booster

By Elaine C R Heckingbottom

Other Books by This Author Available on Kindle include
Richard's Magic Book
Richard's Magical Day Out
Can We Play Maths Today, Please?
Help! Are We Nearly There Yet?
Fantastical Facts for Quizzical Kids
11+ Guide to Figurative Language
11+ Guide to Short Writing Tasks

Soon to be available
WOW! I Can Do It! Book 1
WOW! I Can Do 11+ Comprehensions Book 1
WOW! I Can Do Basic Calculations for the 11+ Book 1

For all the children who have worked with Heckingbottom Learning to prepare for the 11+; whether it was in the past, is in the present, or whether it will be ones that I will work with in the future.

Also, for all of the rest of you who have discovered my resources and are using this book to help you to prepare for that dreaded exam.

Good luck!

Table of Contents

Excerpts from other books by the same author

Note to Parents

Welcome to my Vocabulary Booster Pack, devised from many years of teaching both Year 5 & 6 children and helping to prepare them primarily for the 11+ selection tests and also, to a lesser extent, for the Key Stage 2 SATs.

In today's increasingly competitive society, preparation for the 11+ has become incredibly tough, whichever education authority area you live in – and the benchmarks keep moving; which makes it more confusing for parents to know how best to help their children to prepare. Do you use tutors, or one of the many tutoring clubs or companies that are cropping up more and more in the 11+ areas? Do you try to teach them yourselves, using the many books available – and, if so, which books do you use? Or do you do what many parents are now doing and use a mixture of the above?

As an experienced Year 5 & 6 teacher, I have been helping children (and their parents) to prepare for the 11+ in the Essex area for a great many years now, and can only say that, whichever method you use with your child, you will find that preparation for the 11+ exams will involve studying many concepts that they will not have faced before. Many of the questions are extremely hard, and not all the elements of the exam can be fully prepared for; however, even in the areas of the country where they now claim the exams cannot be 'tutored' for, there are still many tools that you can give your children to help their preparation - and one of the best of those tools is a good working vocabulary. This is beneficial for both the English paper and the Verbal Reasoning Paper, as a range of tricky vocabulary questions frequently crop up in the majority of Verbal Reasoning papers.

A richly varied vocabulary can enhance any child's chances in the 11+ exams; particularly their knowledge of synonyms and antonyms. Words such as ire, irk, wrath, precipice, valour, veto, etc. can crop up regularly both in English and in Verbal Reasoning test; as can homonyms like the word 'minute' (is that minute as in a fraction of an hour, or minute as in tiny?) or refuse (to say no, or rubbish?) You will often need to look at the context to see – but if your children are not aware of the second meaning, they could well find themselves being caught out – especially when they are presented with a list of words out of context.

In addition to this, their knowledge of literary devices such as similes, metaphors, alliteration and parts of speech such as the types of nouns, pronouns, adjectives, adverbs and verbs are also being assessed. There are literally hundreds of games and activities that you can try with your child to develop these skills; several of which are included towards the back of this book; however, these are concepts that we will look at in more depth in further books in this series.

This set of practice questions has been designed to develop the language skills that are an essential tool in a child's preparation for the various different 11+ tests used for entrance to selective schools around the country.

As an experienced Year 5 & 6 teacher, I have based this book on material that I have been using and adapting over a great many years. The key purpose of this book is to help you to enhance your child's vocabulary through frequent short bursts of practice.

Many of the words that I have chosen to use in this book are words that occur in the NFER Practice Verbal Reasoning Tests, in similar practice papers or in past English Papers produced by the Consortium for Selective Schools in Essex (CSSE).

How to use this book

- Getting your child merely to read through the book once (or even twice!) will be of very little benefit. If you want your child to benefit fully from the material enclosed, you would be best advised to work with your child in short bursts. As each page contains, on average, between 8 and 10 puzzles or questions relating to vocabulary (some of which can appear quite complex) between 2 and 6 pages a day should be sufficient if you want your child to learn and absorb the new vocabulary that they encounter there.

- Each page of questions should take around 5 to 10 minutes to complete, working a little like a flashcard, and is followed by its own answer page. Get your child to give their answers, then look at the answer page with them and see if they agree with my answers. Whilst some of the words may seem very simple, this is an important part of building confidence and reinforcing knowledge; however, other words may seem very difficult. Don't be afraid to discuss the ones that your child was unsure of – and make a note of them. Revisit these words on and off over the next week or so, until you are sure that your child is confident with them.

- Because of this, it helps to keep a notebook handy to write down new words or words which have caused problems. Some children may like to highlight unfamiliar words or even like to keep a record of their answers in a notebook; whilst others (particularly those who prefer a more kinaesthetic approach to learning) will prefer to work through the book answering orally. However, whichever method your child prefers, it helps to work with them to ensure that they really are finding the correct answers and trying to develop their skills.

- Don't express frustration or anger when your child doesn't know a word that you come across, even if it's one you've talked about recently. Remember – new words and new concepts have to be experienced four or five times before they move into the long term memory, so work with your child to learn it.

- Write tricky words on a post-it note or a flash card, along with 2 or 3 key synonyms and stick it on the toilet door, where your child will see it several times a day! (This could also lead to interesting discussions with any visitors who may also need to use your loo!). You might also like to add an antonym in a contrasting colour.

- Use a multi-sensual approach to learning new words. Writing them out; saying them aloud; using them in games such as hangman; even writing them big and bold on a patio or drive using an old washing up liquid bottle filled with water all help. Some children may like to develop actions, songs or dances for certain groups of words to help to fix them in their brains. Whatever works best with your child is great – but don't be afraid to try several different methods, just for variety.

- Don't be afraid to go back and revisit sections that you have already covered. Constant revision is a great way to reinforce new vocabulary – children rarely learn or absorb words that they have only seen once or twice, and really benefit from regular revision.

Turn learning vocabulary into a game wherever possible! Several ideas for games and activities to develop vocabulary are included towards the back of this book – many of which require very little preparation and can actually be played in the car on the way to and from school.

- Talk about unfamiliar words and try to use them with your child more and more and, above all, don't be afraid to use more complex vocabulary with your child. Television and modern literature have often been guilty of 'dumbing down' the richness and breadth of the English language; but I strongly believe that children can never be too young to be introduced to trickier, complex vocabulary. Indeed, many of the Year 1 and 2 children in my former school were already confident in their use of words such as 'tepid' and 'indolent'. Because we were not afraid to use these words with them, they were also able to use them confidently, even in their writing, which is fantastic!

- It's never too early to start working on extending your child's vocabulary. You will be amazed at some of the words that they start to use if they are taught to treat unusual vocabulary with confidence!

- It's never too late to be developing your child's vocabulary in the lead up to the dreaded exams. I still remember clearly the fact that, two days before I took my 11+, I learnt a new word – penultimate. I was able to use this in my exam, and was later asked about it in my final entrance interview. To this day, I am convinced that this was one of the key things that got me into my family's chosen school!

One of my pupils this year leant to talk about 'ambrosial aromas' and 'sinuous, monolithic pathways' around a fortnight before his 11+ - and managed to fit both phrases into his writing on the day!

- Use a good quality thesaurus and a good dictionary as a learning tool. These days I find that, rather than recommending a paper format, I tend to recommend an electronic dictionary such as the Seiko Concise Oxford English Dictionary and Thesaurus which, at the time of writing, costs around £45 on Amazon; as this is more fun to use and never seems as onerous as looking up words in a paper dictionary! In addition, the included spell checker, anagram solver and a fantastic games facility allowing your child to store and use new words from their vocabulary and/or their spelling list can all be used in the car as well as at home.

- Above all, make it fun! Children learn far more easily when they are enjoying themselves!

May I take this opportunity to wish you and your children all the best in the tests that they are preparing to take?

GOOD LUCK!

Introductory Pages

These are here to give you a feel of how the book works. Each page is followed by its own answer section, with accompanied explanations or support.

Synonyms are words which are very close in meaning to one another – such as open and ajar; hide and conceal; sleep and doze.
Antonyms are words that are OPPOSITE in meaning to one another – such as open and closed, reveal and conceal, awake and asleep.

Look at the groups of words below and select the **TWO SYNONYMS** (words which are closest in meaning) - one from each set.

a. (perfect, cradle, moon)   (sunshine, baby, faultless)

b. (splash, scrape, new)   (flash, flesh, fresh)

c. (inside, extent, incense)   (outside, interior, outdoors)

d. (thunder, snowstorm, hail)   (sleet, blizzard, lightning)

e. (different, similar, odd)   (alike, even, quiet)

f. (cease, crease, wrinkle)   (stop, start, iron)

g. (solution, excuse, remedy)   (lie, tell, reason)

h. (amaze, astound, maze)   (fun, garden, labyrinth)

i. (drink, drank, drunk)   (water, juice, intoxicated)

The answers!

a. (<u>perfect,</u> cradle, moon)   (sunshine, baby, <u>faultless</u>)

b. (splash, scrape, <u>new</u>)   (flash, flesh, <u>fresh</u>)

c. (<u>inside</u>, extent, incense)   (outside, <u>interior</u>, outdoors)

d. (thunder, <u>snowstorm</u>, hail)   (sleet <u>blizzard,</u> lightning)

e. (different, <u>similar</u>, odd)   (<u>alike</u>, even, quiet)

f. (<u>cease</u>, crease, wrinkle)   (<u>stop,</u> start, iron)

g. (solution, <u>excuse,</u> remedy)   (lie, tell, <u>reason</u>)

h. (amaze, astound, <u>maze</u>)   (fun, garden, <u>labyrinth</u>)

i. (drink, drank, <u>drunk</u>)   (water, juice, <u>intoxicated</u>)

Notes

- The opposite of interior is exterior!
- Whilst hail and sleet are relatively similar in that they are both forms of cold precipitation, snowstorm and blizzard are virtually the same
- Drink, drank, drunk is always a funny one, especially when you look at the way the tenses work. John drinks the wine, John drank the wine; the wine was drunk (and so was John – he was intoxicated!)

Look at the groups of words below and select the **TWO** antonyms (words which are most opposite in meaning) – one from each group.

(hour, small, huge)	(minute, clock, chair)
(loud, expensive, gentle)	(dear, quiet, noise)
(rear, fear, near)	(back, tear, far)
(inside, insect, incapable)	(capable, side, sect)
(swim, float, dive)	(bath, sink, toilet)
(dear, sweetheart, love)	(nice, cheap, expensive)
(few, minority many)	(mostly majority certainly)
(glib timid tiresome)	(fib bold blame)
(foolish ignoramus rude)	(wise known discourteous)

The Answers!

(hour, small, <u>huge</u>)	(<u>minute</u>, clock, chair)
(<u>loud</u>, expensive, gentle)	(dear, <u>quiet</u>, noise)
(rear, fear, <u>near</u>)	(back, tear, <u>far</u>)
(inside, insect, <u>incapable</u>)	(<u>capable</u>, side, sect)
(swim, <u>float</u>, dive)	(bath, <u>sink</u>, toilet)
(<u>dear</u>, sweetheart, love)	(nice, <u>cheap</u>, expensive)
(few, <u>minority</u> many)	(mostly <u>majority</u> certainly)
(glib <u>timid</u> tiresome)	(fib <u>bold</u> blame)
(<u>foolish</u> ignoramus rude)	(<u>wise</u> known discourteous)

The first pair of words on this page causes problems for a great many people, who try to match hour and minute as opposites. Far from being opposites, these are merely different periods of time.

Minute is a homonym. There are two very different ways of pronouncing the word, each of which has a totally different meaning, as in the sentence:

A <u>minute</u> is a <u>minute</u> period of time

- In the first use of the word, it is pronounced 'min-it' and it is a short period of time

- The second time I used the word in the sentence above, you need to pronounce it as 'my-newt' and you have a synonym for miniscule or tiny.

<u>Joke Time!</u>

Although he is not particularly small, I call my pet amphibian 'Tiny' because he is <u>my newt</u>!

Synonyms

Synonyms are groups of words that have similar meanings to one another; such as 'small, tiny, miniature' or 'said, declared, stated' etc.

Can you think of some synonyms for the following words…?

- Large

- Quiet

- Loud

- Notice

- Watch

- Swallow

- Swift

If you've been thinking hard (or using your thesaurus) you will probably have realised that some of these words have more than one meaning. These words are the sort that commonly crop up in a range of 11+ questions, so make sure you are aware of them!

Have a go at these!

Select the two words in each set which are most similar in meaning.

a. skimmer, slimmer, shimmer, stammer, shine

b. clothes, peel, skin, foot, body

c. grizzly, clothed, hidden, bare, naked, bear

d. excursion, excavate, trip, trap, extend

e. sparkle, tinsel, glass, twinkle, cake

f. soldier, battle, brave, courageous, tank

g. bucket, water, pail, pale, bouquet

h. tired, asleep, awake, fatigued, bedtime

i. colour, dim, bright, gloomy, grey

j. run, walk, fast, speed, swift

The answers

a. skimmer, slimmer, <u>shimmer</u>, stammer, <u>shine</u>

b. clothes, <u>peel</u>, <u>skin,</u> foot, body

c. grizzly, clothed, hidden, <u>bare</u>, <u>naked</u>, bear

d. <u>excursion</u>, excavate, <u>trip</u>, trap, extend

e. <u>sparkle</u>, tinsel, glass, <u>twinkle</u>, cake

f. soldier, battle, <u>brave</u>, <u>courageous</u>, tank

g. <u>bucket</u>, water, <u>pail,</u> pale, bouquet

h. <u>tired</u>, asleep, awake, <u>fatigued</u>, bedtime

i. colour, <u>dim</u>, bright, <u>gloomy</u>, grey

j. run, walk, <u>fast</u>, speed, <u>swift</u>

N.B.

b) Peel – think of orange peel. It's the skin of the orange!

c) Whilst a Grizzly is a type of bear, the other 'bare' and 'naked' are a better match, as they actually mean exactly the same thing.

d) Trip is one of those words with a wide range of meanings. Be careful! Remember - an excursion is an outing ... which is another type of trip!

f) Soldiers may have to be brave in battle; but a better synonym for brave would be courageous. Another really good synonym is 'valiant'.

g) I hope you didn't get caught out by the homophones 'pail' and 'pale'! Try to remember which one is which! Can you think of a trick to help you to remember?

h) 'Fatigued' relates to the French word 'fatigué' – which means 'tired'!

j) Whilst 'swift' can mean speedy or fast, it is also the name of a type of bird similar to a swallow.

Select the two words which are most similar in meaning.

a. birthday, presents, Easter, gifts, celebration

b. snow, ice, ocean, glacier, sea

c. sensible, endless, edible, senseless, reliable

d. creature, tree, plant, acorn, animal

e. fly, spin, twirl, dance, float

f. soar, linger, loiter, swipe, swoop

g. proud, haughty, modest, quiet, rapid

h. match, football, judge, tennis, referee

i. merge, blend, separate, change, send

j. trap, confine, reject, restrict, chain

The Answers

a. birthday, <u>presents</u>, Easter, <u>gifts</u>, celebration

b. snow, ice, <u>ocean</u>, glacier, <u>sea</u>

c. <u>sensible</u>, endless, edible, senseless, <u>reliable</u>

d. <u>creature</u>, tree, plant, acorn, <u>animal</u>

e. fly, <u>spin</u>, <u>twirl</u>, dance, float

f. soar, <u>linger</u>, <u>loiter</u>, swipe, swoop

g. <u>proud</u>, <u>haughty</u>, modest, quiet, rapid

h. match, football, <u>judge</u>, tennis, <u>referee</u>

i. <u>merge</u>, <u>blend</u>, separate, change, send

j. trap, <u>confine</u>, reject, <u>restrict</u>, chain

In each of the sets below, select the **TWO** words which are closest in meaning, one from each set.

a. (hot, cold, warm)   (taper, tepid, tapir)

b. (clever, brilliant, intelligent) (slow, sly, shiny)

c. (pursue, peruse, perhaps)   (cheer, cheese, chase)

d. (steep, rocky, climb)   (ascend, descend, sloping)

e. (slip, slide, slither)   (mistake, tread, mud)

f. (beginner, youth, child)   (young, novice, experience)

g. (notice, poster, sticker)   (observe, hear, think)

h. (engine, car, exhaust)   (spark, energy, deplete)

The Answers

a. (hot, cold _warm_)   (taper, _tepid,_ tapir)

b. (clever, _brilliant_, intelligent) (slow, sly, _shiny_)

c. (_pursue_, peruse, perhaps)   (cheer, cheese, _chase_)

d. (steep, rocky, _climb_)   (ascend, descend, sloping)

e. (_slip_, slide, slither)   (_mistake_, tread, mud)

f. (_beginner_, youth, child)   (young, _novice_, experience)

g. (_notice_, poster, sticker)   (_observe_, hear, think)

h. (engine, car, _exhaust_)   (spark, energy, _deplete_)

N.B. Whilst slopes can be steep, that is not true of all slopes.
Some are very shallow.

Look at the groups of words below and select the **TWO** words which have the same, or nearly the same, meaning as the word in capitals.

a. REVOLVE   (turn, return, rotate, shoot, involve)

b. GRAVE   (frivolous, solemn, funeral, severe, angry)

c. FUTILE   (useful, in vain, essential, pointless, vital)

d. ESSENTIAL (imperative, devious, indolent, vital, trivial)

e. START   (stop, finish, begin, commence, continue)

f. SPRING   (wire, autumn, blossom, pounce, bound, rain)

g. PROTEST   (agree, object, flee, challenge, support)

h. PERPLEX   (stumble, astound, amaze, confuse, puzzle)

BE CAREFUL!

One thing that often catches people out with this sort of question is failure to read the question carefully.
My students are all used to being reminded to RTFQC
(Read The Full Question Carefully)
– and, after several errors and reminders, this becomes
RTFQCYT (Read The Flipping Question Carefully You Twit!)

Did you read the question carefully?
Did you make sure you had found TWO words each time?

If so, you can go on to look at the answers.
If not, go back and try again!

The Answers

a. REVOLVE   (<u>turn</u>, return, <u>rotate</u>, shoot, involve)

b. GRAVE   (frivolous, <u>solemn</u>, funeral, <u>severe</u>, angry)

c. FUTILE   (useful, <u>in vain</u>, essential, <u>pointless</u>, vital)

d. ESSENTIAL (<u>imperative</u>, devious, indolent, <u>vital</u>, trivial)

e. START   (stop, finish, <u>begin, commence</u>, continue)

f. SPRING   (wire, autumn, blossom, <u>pounce, bound</u>, rain)

g. PROTEST   (agree, <u>object</u>, flee, <u>challenge</u>, support)

h. PERPLEX   (stumble, astound, amaze, <u>confuse, puzzle</u>)

Some of the trickier words in this section are:

- Grave – this can be a noun or an adjective.

  The noun describes the place where we lay a body at a funeral. Synonyms for this include tomb, catacomb and crypt. There is no opposite.

  The adjective can be thought to describe the way that people look at a funeral – solemn, serious and severe. It can also be used to describe a serious incident or offence.

  Opposites would be frivolous, trivial, and unimportant.

- Essential – it is essential, imperative and vital that you build a good working vocabulary if you want to take the 11+.

- Futile means worthless, pointless, in vain. It would be futile to attempt to take an exam without preparing for it carefully!

- Spring – this can be noun or a verb

  The noun can describe a coil of wire found in many mechanical devices. It has no real synonyms. As a noun, it can also describe the season of the year. Again, it has no real synonyms or antonyms

  As a verb, it describes the action of jumping or bouncing – with loads of great synonyms!

Select the two words in each set which are most similar in meaning.

a. Microscope, small, fragile, tiny, huge

b. Even, number, strange, common, odd

c. Trendy, casual, informal, stylish, wary

d. Cunning, artistic, creative, stylish, artful

e. Irritate, water, annoy, scratch, frustrate

f. Focussed, intelligent, capable, competent, quiet

g. Tidy, cleaner, messy, neater, chaotic

h. Superficial smart, elaborate, shallow, lonely

i. Weigh, heavy, light, balance, stabilise

j. Thirsty, prudent, forty, fifty, thrifty

The Answers

a. Microscope, <u>small</u>, fragile, <u>tiny</u>, huge

b. Even, number, <u>strange</u>, common, <u>odd</u>

c. Trendy, <u>casual</u>, <u>informal</u>, stylish, wary

d. <u>Cunning</u>, artistic, creative, stylish, <u>artful</u>

e. <u>Irritate</u>, water, <u>annoy</u>, scratch, frustrate

f. Focussed, intelligent, <u>capable</u>, <u>competent</u>, quiet

g. Tidy, cleaner, <u>messy</u>, neater, <u>chaotic</u>

h. <u>Superficial</u> smart, elaborate, <u>shallow</u>, lonely

i. Weigh, heavy, light, <u>balance</u>, <u>stabilise</u>

j. Thirsty, <u>prudent</u>, forty, fifty, <u>thrifty</u>

Look at the groups of words below and select the **TWO** words which have the same, or nearly the same, meaning as the word in capitals.

a. DECAY (rot, rock, melt, spoil, improve)

b. EAGER (rush, hurry, keen, lethargic, enthusiastic)

c. ESTIMATE (number, total, calculate, predict, guess)

d. DISPUTE (despair, argue, disagree, lose, agree)

e. INDOLENT (idol, busy, diligent, lazy, idle)

f. LABOUR (manual, work, party, government, strive)

g. IRATE (angry, cry, help, furious, ire)

h. ANGUISH (sorrow, doubt, distress, anxiety, fear)

<u>REMEMBER TO BE CAREFUL!</u>

RTFQCYT

(Read The Flipping Question Carefully, You Twit!)

Did you read the question carefully?
Did you make sure you had found TWO words each time?

If so, you can go on to look at the answers.
If not, go back and try again!

The Answers

a. DECAY   (<u>rot</u>, rock, melt, <u>spoil</u>, improve)

b. EAGER   (rush, hurry, <u>keen</u>, lethargic, <u>enthusiastic</u>)

c. ESTIMATE   (number, total, calculate, <u>predict</u>, <u>guess)</u>

d. DISPUTE   (despair <u>argue</u>, <u>disagree</u>, lose, agree)

e. INDOLENT   (idol, busy, diligent, <u>lazy</u>, <u>idle)</u>

f. LABOUR   (manual, <u>work</u>, party, government, <u>strive)</u>

g. IRATE   (<u>angry</u>, cry, help, <u>furious</u>, ire)

h. ANGUISH   (<u>sorrow</u>, doubt, <u>distress</u>, anxiety, fear)

- Someone who is lethargic will have an extremely laid back attitude to life. A lethargic person is not keen or eager to do well and will enter into things rather half-heartedly. Hopefully, if you have got this far into the book, you do not have a lethargic attitude to learning vocabulary (unless your parents have really had to bribe you to get this far! LOL!)

- Dispute can be an abstract noun or a verb. It can mean an argument or a disagreement, or it can mean the act of arguing.

  E.g. There was a <u>dispute</u> between Britain and Argentina in the 1980s. The two countries <u>disputed</u> the ownership of the Falkland Islands.

- Don't get confused between the homophones 'idol' and 'idle'. An idol is a type of god – something that people might worship or idolise – or a hero, such as a pop idol. 'Idle' means lazy or indolent. Opposites would be hard-working, diligent or industrious.

- Irate is a lovely word, meaning really angry or furious. Ire is an old fashioned word from the same root, meaning extreme anger or wrath.

Can you think of a word that means the same as the first word, but which rhymes with the second one?

a. ASCEND   rhyme

b. FLAVOUR   waist

c. EAGER   queen

d. MELT   straw

e. IDLE   crazy

f. SOLEMN   cave

g. HAUGHTY   loud

h. BRIGHT   briny

i. FEED   wheat

j. BROOK   shiver

k. STREET   code

l. TINY   cute

m. LOCH   snake

n. LOQUACIOUS ratty

The Answers

a.	ASCEND	rhyme	CLIMB
b.	FLAVOUR	waist	TASTE
c.	EAGER	queen	KEEN
d.	MELT	straw	THAW
e.	IDLE	crazy	LAZY
f.	SOLEMN	cave	GRAVE
g.	HAUGHTY	loud	PROUD
h.	BRIGHT	briny	SHINY
i.	FEED	wheat	EAT
j.	BROOK	shiver	RIVER
k.	STREET	code	ROAD
l.	TINY	cute	MINUTE
m.	LOCH	snake	LAKE
n.	LOQUACOIOS	ratty	CHATTY

Select the two words in each set which are most similar in meaning.

a. objective, biased, changed, altar, subjective

b. wall, section, divide, sense, multiply

c. direct, search, hide, explain, describe

d. descend, climb, align, group, fall

e. solid, broad, firm, heavy, sturdy

f. shiver, cold, frozen, frightened, tremble

g. view, belief, state, charity, church

h. harsh, fragile, broken, durable, lasting

i. hasten, funny, listen, speed, annoy

j. deny, accuse, insinuate, guilty, innocent

The Answers.

a. objective, <u>biased</u>, changed, altar, <u>subjective</u>

b. wall, <u>section</u>, <u>divide</u>, sense, multiply

c. direct, search, hide, <u>explain</u>, <u>describe</u>

d. <u>descend</u>, climb, align, group, <u>fall</u>

e. <u>solid</u>, broad, firm, heavy, <u>sturdy</u>

f. <u>shiver</u>, cold, frozen, frightened, <u>tremble</u>

g. <u>view</u>, <u>belief</u>, state, charity, church

h. harsh, fragile, broken, <u>durable</u>, <u>lasting</u>

i. <u>hasten</u>, funny, listen, <u>speed</u>, annoy

j. deny, <u>accuse</u>, <u>insinuate</u>, guilty, innocent

Look for the TWO words in the brackets which have the SAME or nearly the same meaning as the word in capitals outside the brackets.

E.g.   ASSEMBLE   (committee, <u>collect,</u> model, <u>gather,</u> kit)

1. REMEDY   (hospital, patient, cure, doctor, solution)

2. PURCHASE   (package, shop, buy, prohibit, acquire)

3. ODOUR   (odious, occur, smell, fragrance, order)

4. NIMBLE   (agile, stiff, aerobic, spry, weak)

5. ROBUST   (resort, vigorous, vulnerable, strong, metal)

6. NECESSARY (essential, vigour, imperative, convey, frantic)

7. ROTATE   (ration, revolve, mower, gyrate, circumference)

8. BARREN   (desolate, desert, Lord, Earl, empty)

9. DECEIVE   (hijack, betray, jest, delude, joke)

10. TEMERITY   (timidity, audacity, nerve, nervous, care)

The Answers.

E.g. ASSEMBLE (committee, <u>collect,</u> model, <u>gather,</u> kit)

1. REMEDY (hospital, patient, <u>cure,</u> doctor, <u>solution</u>)

2. PURCHASE (package, shop, <u>buy,</u> prohibit, <u>acquire</u>)

3. ODOUR (odious, occur, <u>smell, fragrance,</u> order)

4. NIMBLE (<u>agile,</u> stiff, aerobic, <u>spry,</u> weak)

5. ROBUST (resort, <u>vigorous,</u> vulnerable, <u>strong,</u> metal)

6. NECESSARY (<u>essential,</u> vigour, <u>imperative,</u> convey, frantic)

7. ROTATE (ration, <u>revolve,</u> mower, <u>gyrate,</u> circumference)

8. BARREN (<u>desolate,</u> desert, Lord, Earl, <u>empty</u>)

9. DECEIVE (hijack, <u>betray,</u> jest, <u>delude,</u> joke)

10. TEMERITY (timidity, <u>audacity, nerve,</u> nervous, care)

Use your thesaurus to find a simple, three letter word that means the same, or nearly the same as each of these longer words.

a. gigantic

b. as well

c. melancholy

d. curve

e. portion

f. rupture

g. grievous

h. anger

The Answers (You may think of others too!)

a. gigantic   BIG

b. as well   TOO

c. melancholy   SAD

d. curve   ARC

e. portion   BIT

f. rupture   RIP or POP or CUT

g. grievous   BAD

h. anger   IRE, IRK or VEX

Unjumble the letters to find a **synonym** for each of the words in capitals.

a. trotae   TURN

b. blimne   AGILE

c. vimprteeai   ESSENTIAL

d. vencoy   TRANSPORT

e. bndnaao   DESERT

f. xtrreeio   OUTSIDE

g. rbthiiop   BAN

h. lgniidet   INDUSTRIOUS

i. veduois   SLY

j. ddleeu   CHEAT

k. eeauprptl   PERMANANT

l. brouts   STRONG

m. rpuaechs   BUY

The Answers.

a. trotae   TURN   ROTATE

b. blimne   AGILE   NIMBLE

c. vimprteeai   ESSENTIAL   IMPERATIVE

d. vencoy   TRANSPORT   CONVEY

e. bndnaao   DESERT   ABANDON

f. xtrreeio   OUTSIDE   EXTERIOR

g. rbthiiop   BAN   PROHIBIT

h. lgniidet   INDUSTRIOUS   DILIGENT

i. veduois   SLY   DEVIOUS

j. ddleeu   CHEAT   DELUDE

k. eeauprptl   PERMANANT   PERPETUAL

l. brouts   STRONG   ROBUST

m. rpuaechs   BUY   PURCHASE

Find the three words in each set that are most closely related in meaning.

a. tired, weary, content, fatigued, tried

b. embark, journey, sail, voyage, trip

c. unusual, strange, normal, average, peculiar

d. truth, pretend, try, bluff, feign

e. befriend, astonish, humiliate, embarrass, disconcert

f. crave, desire, heartfelt, long, short

g. rubbish, veto, refuse, litter, toilet

h. disagree, opposite, flatter, compliment, adulate

i. pine, pledge, promise, hedge, covenant

j. imply, allude, trivial, petty, insinuate,

k. negligent, careless, carefree, able, indifferent

l. turbulent, vicious, viscous, violent, violet

The Answers.

a. <u>tired</u>, <u>weary</u>, content, <u>fatigued</u>, tried

b. embark, <u>journey</u>, sail, <u>voyage</u>, <u>trip</u>

c. <u>unusual</u>, <u>strange</u>, normal, average, <u>peculiar</u>

d. truth, <u>pretend</u>, try, <u>bluff</u>, <u>feign</u>

e. befriend, astonish, <u>humiliate</u>, <u>embarrass</u>, <u>disconcert</u>

f. <u>crave</u>, <u>desire</u>, heartfelt, <u>long</u>, short

g. <u>rubbish</u>, veto, <u>refuse</u>, <u>litter</u>, cat

h. disagree, opposite, <u>flatter</u>, <u>compliment</u>, <u>adulate</u>

i. pine, <u>pledge</u>, <u>promise</u>, hedge, <u>covenant</u>

j. <u>imply</u>, <u>allude</u>, trivial, petty, <u>insinuate</u>,

k. <u>negligent</u>, <u>careless</u>, carefree, able, <u>indifferent</u>

l. <u>turbulent</u>, <u>vicious</u>, viscous, <u>violent</u>, violet

Tricky Synonym Questions

Some words, as we know, have very varied meanings, and one of the results of this is a certain type of question that can be quite tricky.

e.g. Find the ONE word from the top list that can have a similar meaning to the words in the two sets of brackets

FUTILE GRAVE TOMB CRITICAL GLOOMY

(CATACOMB CRYPT)   (SOLEMN SERIOUS)

THE TRICK is to look at the first pair of words and compare them with the words on the top row. You should be able to rule out some of the words straight away – for example, futile, critical and gloomy do NOT mean the same as catacomb and crypt. Once you have done this, look at the second pair of words and compare them ONLY with the words that you HAVE NOT ALREADY DISCOUNTED. Tomb does NOT mean the same as solemn and serious, but grave does.

Therefore, although some of the words can mean the same as the words in ONE of the sets of brackets, the only word that matches all four words in both sets of brackets is GRAVE, so this must be the answer.

Try this one!

TRASH   REFUSE   VETO   WITHHOLD   GARBAGE

(LITTER   RUBBISH)   (ABSTAIN   DECLINE)

Hopefully, you remembered that REFUSE is a homonym; with two ways of pronouncing it and two totally different meanings – and chose that one.

Here are another couple of questions to have a go at.

Find the ONE word from the top list that can have a similar meaning to the words in the two sets of brackets

GENTLE CANDY NICE SWEET LOVING

(SUGARY SYRUPY) (LOVELY KIND)

MUSICAL PLAY THEATRE SHOW ACTOR

(DRAMA PRODUCTION) (ROMP FROLIC)

The answers

GENTLE CANDY NICE <u>SWEET</u> LOVING

(SUGARY SYRUPY) (LOVELY KIND)

MUSICAL <u>PLAY</u> THEATRE SHOW ACTOR

(DRAMA PRODUCTION) (ROMP FROLIC)

<u>Now try these</u>

Find the ONE word from the top list that can have a similar meaning to the words in the two sets of brackets

STRAIGHT SIMPLE HARD DIFFICULT TRIVIAL

(PLAIN NATURAL)   (EASY CLEAR)

ASK PAST RECEIVE PRESENT FUTURE

(NOW CURRENT) (GIVE OFFER)

BANNER SCRIBE WRITE SIGN NOTIFY

(AUTOGRAPH INITIAL)   (NOTICE POSTER)

GROUP KEEP DIVISION GENTLE KIND

(TENDER NICE)   (TYPE SORT)

The Answers

STRAIGHT <u>SIMPLE</u> HARD DIFFICULT TRIVIAL

(PLAIN NATURAL) (EASY CLEAR)

ASK PAST RECEIVE <u>PRESENT</u> FUTURE

(NOW CURRENT) (GIVE OFFER)

BANNER SCRIBE WRITE <u>SIGN</u> NOTIFY

(AUTOGRAPH INITIAL) (NOTICE POSTER)

GROUP KEEP DIVISION GENTLE <u>KIND</u>

(TENDER NICE) (TYPE SORT)

Find the ONE word from the top list that can have a similar meaning to the words in the two sets of brackets

MUSCLE   TIN   ENERGY   MIGHT   MAYBE

(POWER   STRENGTH)   (MAY   CAN)

STREAM   DRIP   FALL   DROP   LOWER

(TRICKLE   GLOBULE)   (DECLINE   DECREASE)

CREASE   FLAP   ENVELOPE   SIGN   SEA

(WAVE   FLUTTER)   (TAB   FOLD)

OFFICE   COMPANY   BRANCH   FARM   STABLE

(FIRM   STEADY)   (SHED   BARN)

The Answers

MUSCLE TIN ENERGY <u>MIGHT</u> MAYBE

(POWER STRENGTH) (MAY CAN)

STREAM DRIP FALL <u>DROP</u> LOWER

(TRICKLE GLOBULE) (DECLINE DECREASE)

CREASE <u>FLAP</u> ENVELOPE SIGN SEA

(WAVE FLUTTER) (TAB FOLD)

OFFICE COMPANY BRANCH FARM <u>STABLE</u>

(FIRM STEADY) (SHED BARN)

In each question below, there are two pairs of words. You must find a word from the list that will go EQUALLY WELL with either pair.

LOOK NOTICE OBSERVE PROMOTION DIRECTION

(SPOT SEE) (ADVERTISEMENT POSTER)

AIM POINT DREAM ASPIRATION LOCATION

(TARGET PINPOINT) (AMBITION OBJECTIVE)

PRICE HURRY CHARGE HIT BILL

(FEE COST) (ATTACK RUSH)

VICTORIOUS BETRAYED SLAPPED LOST BEATEN

(DEFEATED CONQUERED) (STRUCK HIT)

The Answers

LOOK <u>NOTICE</u> OBSERVE PROMOTION DIRECTION

(SPOT SEE) (ADVERTISEMENT POSTER)

<u>AIM</u> POINT DREAM ASPIRATION LOCATION

(TARGET PINPOINT) (AMBITION OBJECTIVE)

PRICE HURRY <u>CHARGE</u> HIT BILL

(FEE COST) (ATTACK RUSH)

VICTORIOUS BETRAYED SLAPPED LOST <u>BEATEN</u>

(DEFEATED CONQUERED) (STRUCK HIT)

In each question below, there are two pairs of words. You must find a word from the list that will go EQUALLY WELL with either pair.

BRIGHT   GOOD   FINE   GREAT   SUNNY

(LOVELY, NICE) (DRY, CLEAR)

SPIN   SNACK   TWIRL   ROLL   CIRCLE

(TURN, REVOLVE)   (BUN, BREAD)

ROSE   SOARED   BLOOM   FLOATED   RED

(BLUSH PINK)   (ASCENDED LIFTED)

RIGID   COMPLEX   STIFF   TROUBLESOME   HARD

(FIRM SOLID)   (DIFFICULT AWKWARD)

<u>The Answers</u>

BRIGHT GOOD <u>FINE</u> GREAT SUNNY

(LOVELY, NICE) (DRY, CLEAR)

SPIN SNACK TWIRL <u>ROLL</u> CIRCLE

(TURN, REVOLVE) (BUN, BREAD)

<u>ROSE</u> SOARED BLOOM FLOATED RED

(BLUSH PINK) (ASCENDED LIFTED)

(Pink wine is referred to as blush, rose or rosé)

RIGID COMPLEX STIFF TROUBLESOME <u>HARD</u>

(FIRM SOLID) (DIFFICULT AWKWARD)

(Recently, I had a rather pedantic child in my class who, whenever one of the others complained that the work was hard, banged on the table and said 'No. This is hard. The work is merely difficult!')

Choose the word that has a similar meaning to the words in both sets of brackets.

WRONG MISTAKE PUZZLE BAFFLE SLIP

(ERROR FAULT)   (MUDDLE CONFUSE)

LOCK ADJOINING CLOSE SEAL NEAR

(NEIGHBOURING ADJACENT)   (SHUT SECURE)

OBJECT MOTIVE AIM THING GADGET

(ARTICLE ITEM)   (GOAL END)

NOD BRAID BOW STRING STOOP

(RIBBON BOW)   (BEND CURTSEY)

WRONG <u>MISTAKE</u> PUZZLE BAFFLE SLIP

(ERROR FAULT) (MUDDLE CONFUSE)

LOCK ADJOINING <u>CLOSE</u> SEAL NEAR

(NEIGHBOURING ADJACENT) (SHUT SECURE)

<u>OBJECT</u> MOTIVE AIM THING GADGET

(ARTICLE ITEM) (GOAL END)

NOD BRAID <u>BOW</u> STRING STOOP

(RIBBON BOW) (BEND CURTSEY)

Choose the word from the top row that has a similar meaning to the words in both sets of brackets

WORLD SOIL MUD EARTH WARREN

(ORB GLOBE)   (DEN SETT)

PRAIRIE CLEAR FIELD DISTINCT PLAIN

(GRASSLAND FLATLAND)   (SIMPLE OBVIOUS)

MINE BLAST MISSILE TRENCH DITCH

(EXCAVATE QUARRY)   (BOMB EXPLOSIVE)

JOB FUNCTION BALL SOCIAL UTILITY

(USE PURPOSE)   (EVENT PARTY)

The Answers

WORLD SOIL MUD <u>EARTH</u> WARREN

(ORB GLOBE)   (DEN SETT)

PRAIRIE CLEAR FIELD DISTINCT <u>PLAIN</u>

(GRASSLAND FLATLAND)   (SIMPLE OBVIOUS)

<u>MINE</u> BLAST MISSILE TRENCH DITCH

(EXCAVATE QUARRY)   (BOMB EXPLOSIVE)

JOB <u>FUNCTION</u> BALL SOCIAL UTILITY

(USE PURPOSE)   (EVENT PARTY)

Antonyms

As I already mentioned at the beginning of this book, antonyms are pairs of words that have opposite meanings; such as open and shut; interior and exterior; ascend and descend.

- How many pairs of antonyms can you think of?

- Try to think of at least 20 pairs before you move on to the next page.

- What is the best pair of antonyms that you can think of?

- Look in your thesaurus to see how to find antonyms there. They are usually at the bottom of the section or, if you have an electronic thesaurus, at the bottom of the 'page'.

More Antonyms

Find the TWO words, one from each group, which are most opposite in meaning.

a. (extra, special, more)   (even, peculiar, ordinary)

b. (fall, float, drift)   (swim, sink, scuttle)

c. (stairs, down, ground)   (climb, up, under)

d. (day, moon, star)   (light, beam, night)

e. (increase, grow, stretch)   (plant, crease, reduce)

f. (dawn, early, wake)   (late, stop, sunrise)

g. (fat, short, slim)   (strong, heavy, tall)

h. (discover, find, treasure)   (lose, trail, loose)

i. (aunt, old, cousin)   (relations, family, young)

j. (reduce, sale, market)   (bargain, increase, shopping)

The Answers

a. (extra, _special,_ more)   (even, peculiar, _ordinary_)

b. (fall, _float,_ drift)   (swim, _sink_, scuttle)

c. (stairs, _down,_ ground)   (climb, _up_, under)

d. (_day_, moon, star)   (light, beam, _night_)

e. (_increase_, grow, stretch)   (plant, crease, _reduce_)

f. (_dawn_, early, wake)   (late, stop, _sunrise_)

g. (fat, _short,_ slim)   (strong, heavy, _tall_)

h. (discover, _find_, treasure)   (_lose_, trail, loose)

i. (aunt, _old_, cousin)   (relations, family, _young_)

j. (_reduce_, sale, market)   (bargain, _increase_, shopping)

Be careful with the difference between loose and lose. The double letters act as a clue!

You will lose a loose tooth if you wobble it too much

Look at the groups of words below and select one word from those in the second box which is opposite in meaning to the word in capitals.

a. WIDE   (broad, vague, long, narrow, motorway)

b. RELIABLE (good, relation, untrustworthy, friend, bad)

c. HEALTHY (strong, energetic, medicine, ill, hospital)

d. DILUTED (watered, cocktail, concentrated, cordial, drink)

e. KIND   (generous, dishonest, lazy, thoughtful, cruel)

f. CAUTIOUS (careful, warning, heedless, lazy, devious)

g. ALWAYS   (each, sometimes, seldom, never, rarely)

h. INTERIOR (inside, exterior, decorator, exit, entrance)

The Answers

   a. WIDE   (broad, vague, long, <u>narrow</u>, motorway)

   b. RELIABLE (good, relation, <u>untrustworthy</u>, friend, bad)

   c. HEALTHY (strong, energetic, medicine, <u>ill</u>, hospital)

   d. DILUTED (watered, cocktail, <u>concentrated</u>, cordial, drink)

   e. KIND   (generous, dishonest, lazy, thoughtful, <u>cruel</u>)

   f. CAUTIOUS (careful, warning, <u>heedless,</u> lazy, devious)

   g. ALWAYS   (each, sometimes, seldom, <u>never</u>, rarely)

   h. INTERIOR (inside, <u>exterior</u>, decorator, exit, entrance)

Be careful with always, sometimes, seldom, never, occasionally.
They catch people out regularly!

Look up a range of synonyms for each word and learn them!

Look at the lists below and select the two words which are most opposite in meaning from each group.

a. write, rite, sinister, right, wrong

b. gift, present, correct, abstract, absent

c. interim, interior, external, interval, exterior

d. descend, depart, devour, ascend, scent

e. generous, represent, mean, average, involve,

f. unite, join, match, separate, equal

g. decrease, inhale, bigger, crease, increase

h. hurry, accident, patient, hasten, impatient

i. rude, indolent, insult, courteous, manners

j. contain, pour, poor, full, empty

The Answers

a. write, rite, sinister, <u>right</u>, <u>wrong</u>

b. gift, <u>present</u>, correct, abstract, <u>absent</u>

c. interim, <u>interior</u>, external, interval, <u>exterior</u>

d. <u>descend</u>, depart, devour, <u>ascend</u>, scent

e. <u>generous</u>, represent, <u>mean</u>, average, involve,

f. <u>unite</u>, fix, match, <u>separate</u>, equal

g. <u>decrease</u>, inhale, bigger, crease, <u>increase</u>

h. hurry, accident, <u>patient</u>, hasten, <u>impatient</u>

i. <u>rude</u>, indolent, insult, <u>courteous</u>, manners

j. contain, pour, poor, <u>full</u>, <u>empty</u>

Use a thesaurus to help you to find an antonym for each of these words from the list below.
WARNING: - there are a few 'red herrings' in the list (i.e. some words which you won't need)

a. absence

b. solid

c. tame

d. commence

e. conceal

f. permanent

g. more

h. youth

i. innocent

j. opaque

<u>Choose from</u>:-

transparent, separate, success, reveal, temporary, wild, guilty, liquid, expensive, conclude, age, presence, less, definite.

The Answers.

a. Absence   PRESENCE

b. solid   LIQUID

c. tame   WILD

d. commence   CONCLUDE

e. conceal   REVEAL

f. permanent   TEMPORARY

g. more   LESS

h. youth   OLD-AGE

i. innocent   GUILTY

j. opaque   TRANSPARENT

Choose from :-

transparent, separate, success, reveal, temporary, wild, guilty, liquid, expensive, conclude, old-age, presence, less, definite.

Select the two words in each group which are most opposite in meaning.

a. dark, light, night, moon, star

b. shine, light, beam, fire, ice

c. fast, type, quick, kind, cruel

d. fox, day, vixen, river, night

e. Friday, August, Summer, Winter, Tuesday

f. kind, caring, considerate, unkind, naughty

g. proud, argumentative, modest, lonely, quiet

h. medium, rare, few, common, over-done

i. tie, extend, adapt, unite, separate

j. odd, strange, sensible, peculiar, even

<u>The Answers</u>.

a. <u>dark</u>, <u>light</u>, night, moon, star

b. shine, light, beam, <u>fire</u>, <u>ice</u>

c. fast, type, quick, <u>kind</u>, <u>cruel</u>

d. fox, <u>day</u>, vixen, river, <u>night</u>

e. Friday, August, <u>Summer</u>, <u>Winter</u>, Tuesday

f. <u>kind</u>, caring, considerate, <u>unkind</u>, naughty

g. <u>proud</u>, argumentative, <u>modest</u>, lonely, quiet

h. medium, <u>rare</u>, few, <u>common</u>, over-done

i. tie, extend, adapt, <u>unite</u>, <u>separate</u>

j. <u>odd</u>, strange, sensible, peculiar, <u>even</u>

Use a thesaurus to help you to find an antonym for each of these words from the list below

a. black

b. difficult

c. entrance

d. buy

e. clean

f. familiar

g. wither

h. join

i. retreat

j. often

Choose from:-

flourish, exit, sever, strange, singular, kindness, none, advance, seldom, easy, dirty, depth, white, sell.

The Answers

a. black   WHITE

b. difficult   EASY

c. entrance   EXIT

d. buy   SELL

e. clean   DIRTY

f. familiar   STRANGE

g. wither   FLOURISH

h. join   SEVER

i. retreat   ADVANCE

j. often   SELDOM

Choose from:-

flourish, exit, sever, strange, singular, kindness, none, advance, seldom, easy, dirty, depth, white, sell.

Replace the word in brackets with an antonym so that the sentence means the opposite.

a. The train (departed) .... on time.

b. The small boy was very (weak) ....

c. The woman was full of (hatred) ....

d. The magician (concealed) .... the rabbit.

e. The (interior) .... of the house was badly decorated.

f. The prisoner was found (guilty) .... of the crime.

g. The attempt to reach the summit was a (failure) ....

h. John turned out to be my (enemy) ....

i. It was a very (broad) .... street.

j. John was a (reckless) .... boy.

k. It was a (tranquil) .... place to have a picnic.

l. After a while, he began to feel (better) ....

m. Peter always arrives (early) ....

Here are my suggestions for the answers. You may come up with others but, if so, you should check them carefully in your thesaurus.

a. The train (departed) ARRIVED on time.

b. The small boy was very (weak) STRONG.

c. The woman was full of (hatred) LOVE.

d. The magician (concealed) REVEALED the rabbit.

e. The (interior) EXTERIOR of the house was badly decorated.

f. The prisoner was found (guilty) INNOCENT of the crime.

g. The attempt to reach the summit was a (failure) SUCCESS.

h. John turned out to be my (enemy) FRIEND.

i. It was a very (broad) NARROW street.

j. John was a (reckless) CAREFUL boy.

k. It was a (tranquil) BUSY/NOISY place to have a picnic.

l. After a while, he began to feel (better) WORSE.

m. Peter always arrives (early) LATE.

Look at the lists below and select the two words which are most opposite in meaning from each group.

a. frightened, strength, failure, sanitary, success.

b. advance, adhere, admit, repeat, retreat

c. arrival, abandon, attract, departure, visit

d. beautiful, scared, scarce, plentiful, graceful

e. permit, forbid, influence, credit, collect

f. contact, contain, conceal, repeal, reveal

g. danger dagger, safely, safety. Knife

h. claim, accuse, quarrel, fight, defend

i. tropical, deserted, humid, arid, barren

j. amplify, elaborate, muffle, restrain, restrict,

The Answers

a. frightened, strength, _failure_, sanitary, _success_.

b. _advance_, adhere, admit, repeat, _retreat_

c. _arrival_, abandon, attract, _departure_, visit

d. beautiful, scared, _scarce_, _plentiful_, graceful

e. _permit_, _forbid_, influence, credit, collect

f. contact, contain, _conceal_, repeal, _reveal_

g. _danger_ dagger, safely, _safety_. knife

h. claim, _accuse_, quarrel, fight, _defend_

i. tropical, deserted, _humid_, _arid_, barren

j. _amplify_, elaborate, _muffle_, restrain, restrict,

Can you think of a word that is opposite in meaning to the word in capitals and rhymes with the word beside it.

a. BRIGHT   bark

b. FAST   go

c. RICH   sure

d. SHARP   grunt

e. OLD   stung

f. SMART   fluffy

g. INTERESTED   afford

h. SLOW   aghast

i. CLOUDY   money

j. DILIGENT   crazy

k. ANGER   fire

The Answers.

a.	BRIGHT	bark	DARK
b.	FAST	go	SLOW
c.	RICH	sure	POOR
d.	SHARP	grunt	BLUNT
e.	OLD	stung	YOUNG
f.	SMART	fluffy	SCRUFFY
g.	INTERESTED	afford	BORED
h.	SLOW	aghast	FAST
i.	CLOUDY	money	SUNNY
j.	DILIGENT	crazy	LAZY
k.	ANGER	fire	IRE

Find the antonym in each set for the word on the left.

DIRTY	muddy, clean, grubby, big, futile
HIGH	foolish, wide, up, drop, low
FOOLISH	wise, silly, neat, wet, red
POLITE	sensible, rude, nice, clever, easy
GENTLE	painful, caring, calm, rough, tender
HUMBLE	proud, down, huge, tall, modest
WEAK	strong, feeble, full, tidy, clumsy
BOILING	empty, dark, freezing, cold, safe

The Answers.

DIRTY	muddy, <u>clean,</u> grubby, big, futile
HIGH	foolish, wide, up, drop, <u>low</u>
FOOLISH	<u>wise,</u> silly, neat, wet, red
POLITE	sensible, <u>rude</u>, nice, clever, easy
GENTLE	painful, caring, calm, <u>rough,</u> tender
HUMBLE	<u>proud,</u> down, huge, tall, modest
WEAK	<u>strong,</u> feeble, full, tidy, clumsy
BOILING	empty, dark, <u>freezing,</u> cold, safe

Use a thesaurus to help you to find an antonym for each of these words from the list below.
WARNING: - there are a few 'red herrings' in the list (i.e. some words which you won't need)

a. Cheap

b. Failure

c. Unite

d. Vague

e. height

f. cruelty

g. all

h. plural

i. seldom

j. sparse

Choose from: - *expensive abundant depth separate singular kindness success definite few none always frequently*

The Answers

    a. cheap   EXPENSIVE

    b. failure   SUCCESS

    c. unite   SEPARATE

    d. vague   DEFINITE

    e. height   DEPTH

    f. cruelty   KINDNESS

    g. all   NONE

    h. plural   SINGULAR

    i. seldom   FREQUENTLY

    j. sparse   ABUNDANT

Unjumble the letters to find an **antonym** for each of the words in capitals.

a. pesraaet   UNITE

b. staboluf   HUMBLE

c. ncclaeo   REVEAL

d. lfwo   EBB

e. ldsmoe   FREQUENTLY

f. guvae   CLEAR

g. pproaev   CONDEMN

h. dolenint   HARD WORKING

i. dibrof   ALLOW

j. ccndloue   COMMENCE

The Answers.

a. pesraaet   UNITE   SEPARATE

b. staboluf   HUMBLE   BOASTFUL

c. ncclaeo   REVEAL   CONCEAL

d. lfwo   EBB   FLOW

e. ldsmoe   FREQUENTLY   SELDOM

f. guvae   CLEAR   VAGUE

g. pproaev   CONDEMN   APPROVE

h. dolenint   HARD WORKING   INDOLENT

i. dibrof   ALLOW   FORBID

j. ccndloue   COMMENCE   CONCLUDE

The Tricky Ones

Sometimes, just to be awkward or to complicate matters, they ask you to give a synonym AND an antonym for a key word.

E.g. Underline TWO words in the brackets, ONE of which has a SIMILAR meaning to the word in capitals and ONE which is OPPOSITE in meaning.

      FIRM   (calm, tired, big, weak, vigorous numerous)

Ask yourself – what does firm mean? It means hard, solid, strong, firm.

Can you think of any other synonyms?

Now look at the options that have been given to you. Compare the word that they have given with each word in turn.

1. FIRM calm – Calm means peaceful. No match

2. FIRM tired - Tired means sleepy. No match

3. FIRM big – no real match. They do NOT mean the same. You can be firm without being big!

4. FIRM weak. Weak is the opposite of strong. If firm and strong are the same, is it possible that firm could be the opposite? YES!

5. FIRM vigorous – similar. Something that is vigorous is something that is strong and powerful.

6. FIRM numerous. Numerous means plentiful. No match.

Here, firm and weak are opposites; firm and vigorous are synonyms; and so you should select BOTH words.

Here you must select **TWO** words in the second section, one of which has the **SAME** or nearly the same meaning as the word in capitals; the other must be **OPPOSITE** in meaning.

a. NUMEROUS   more, many, none, few, some

b. PERMANENT   temporary, evasive, perpetual, wave, now

c. VAGUE   pale, clear, empty, slight, uncertain

d. OFTEN   always, seldom, never, frequently, now

e. HOLLOW   egg, solid, hole, whole, empty

f. CONDEMN   impel, conflict, conduct, blame, approve

g. COMPULSORY   optional, desirable, mandatory, slow, claimed

h. WEALTHY   affluent, needy, sad, influential, pitiful

The Answers

Did you RTFQC? Did you make sure you found two words each time; an antonym AND a synonym?

i.   NUMEROUS   more, <u>many,</u> none, <u>few</u>, some

j.   PERMANENT   <u>temporary</u>, evasive, <u>perpetual</u>, wave, now

k.   VAGUE   pale, <u>clear</u>, empty, slight, <u>uncertain</u>

l.   OFTEN   always, <u>seldom</u>, never, <u>frequently,</u> now

m.   HOLLOW   egg, <u>solid</u>, hole, whole, <u>empty</u>

n.   CONDEMN   impel, conflict, conduct, <u>blame, approve</u>

o.   COMPULSORY   <u>optional,</u> desirable, <u>mandatory</u>, slow, claimed

p.   WEALTHY   <u>affluent, needy</u>, sad, influential, pitiful

Select TWO words from the words in the brackets. ONE must have the SAME or nearly the same meaning as the word in capitals; the other must be OPPOSITE in meaning.

a. STUBBORN   (horse, mule, obstinate, flexible, stain)

b. TRANSPARENT (glass, clear, opposite, opaque, cellophane)

c. TRANQUIL   (peaceful, country, cottage, noisy, busy)

d. VACANT   (flat, occupied, stare, empty, holiday)

e. ABANDON   (quit, ship, stay, island inhabit)

f. CONCEAL   (surprise, hide, convey, reveal, replenish)

g. ENEMY   (battle, friend, invade, foe, endeavour)

h. EXTERIOR (paint, outside, exterminate, interior, inferior)

i. HONEST   (genuine, ignorant, untruthful, rude, courteous)

j. ANCIENT   (decaying, antique, old, dirty, modern)

The Answers.

a. STUBBORN (horse, mule, <u>obstinate, flexible</u>, stain)

b. TRANSPARENT (glass, <u>clear,</u> opposite, <u>opaque</u>, cellophane)

c. TRANQUIL (<u>peaceful,</u> country, cottage, <u>noisy</u>, busy)

d. VACANT (flat, <u>occupied</u>, stare, <u>empty,</u> holiday)

e. ABANDON (<u>quit,</u> ship, <u>stay,</u> island inhabit)

f. CONCEAL (surprise, <u>hide</u>, convey, <u>reveal,</u> replenish)

g. ENEMY (battle, <u>friend,</u> invade, <u>foe,</u> endeavour)

h. EXTERIOR (paint, <u>outside</u>, exterminate, <u>interior</u>, inferior)

i. HONEST (<u>genuine,</u> ignorant, <u>untruthful</u>, rude, courteous)

j. ANCIENT (decaying, antique, <u>old</u>, dirty, <u>modern</u>)

(Whilst antiques are old, not everything that is old or ancient can be called an antique!)

Select TWO words from the words in the brackets. ONE must have the SAME or nearly the same meaning as the word in capitals; the other must be OPPOSITE in meaning.

a. PROHIBIT (private, allow, forbid, provide, trespass)

b. PECULIAR (extinct, extract, odd, usual, pedantic)

c. AID (hospital, assist, anxiety, obstruct, obstreperous)

d. DILIGENT (helpful, indolent, industrious, wary, peaceful)

e. COMMENCE (begin, allow, carry, attempt, conclude)

f. PLENTIFUL (sufficient, ample, feeble, scarce, barren)

g. REGULARLY (frequently, sometimes, never, occasionally)

h. DETERIORATE (undermine, decline, correct, improve)

i. CEASE (ban, prevent, commence, conclude, abolish)

j. BRAVE (strong, weak, cowardly, shy, valiant)

The Answers

a. PROHIBIT   (private, <u>allow, forbid</u>, provide, trespass)

b. PECULIAR   (extinct, extract, <u>odd, usual</u>, pedantic)

c. AID   (hospital, <u>assist</u>, anxiety, <u>obstruct</u>, obstreperous)

d. DILIGENT   (helpful, <u>indolent, industrious</u>, wary, peaceful)

e. COMMENCE   (<u>begin</u>, allow, carry, attempt, <u>conclude</u>)

f. PLENTIFUL   (sufficient, <u>ample</u>, feeble, <u>scarce</u>, barren)

g. REGULARLY   (<u>frequently</u>, sometimes, never, <u>occasionally</u>)

h. DETERIORATE   (undermine, <u>decline</u>, correct, <u>improve</u>)

i. CEASE   (ban, prevent, <u>commence</u>, <u>conclude</u>, abolish)

j. BRAVE   (strong, weak, <u>cowardly</u>, shy, <u>valiant</u>)

Additional Language Based Activities

Homophones and Homonyms

Homophones are words that sound the same as one another but are spelt differently. They crop up frequently in vocabulary type questions, and need to be watched out for.

Find the correct homophones in each of the following sentences

a) The doctor's (practise/practice) is in Warwick Road

b) They (practise/practice) judo every week.

c) The (principle/principal) of the college taught abroad.

d) It was a matter of (principal/principle) that he should write the letter

e) Where is (their/there) rabbit?

f) I put it over (there/their)

g) The (coarse/course) of the river meanders through the field

h) The material he used was very (coarse/course)

i) The strong (currants/currents) pulled the canoes towards the rapids

j) Mum used (currants/currents) in the Hot Cross Buns

k) The train was (stationary/stationery) in the station.

l) I bought my new pencil from the (stationary/stationery) shop

Find the correct homophones in each of the following sentences

a) The doctor's (practise/<u>practice</u>) is in Warwick Road *(noun)*

b) They (<u>practise</u>/practice) judo every week. *(verb)*

c) The (principle/<u>principal</u>) of the college taught abroad. *(a person can be a pal!)*

d) It was a matter of (principal/<u>principle</u>) that he should write the letter *(not a person, so not a pal!)*

e) Where is (<u>their</u>/there) rabbit? *(belonging to them)*

f) I put it over (<u>there</u>/their). *(here is a place – so is there!)*

g) The (coarse/<u>course</u>) of the river meanders through the field

h) The material he used was very (<u>coarse</u>/course)

i) The strong (currants/<u>currents</u>) pulled the canoes towards the rapids. *(Currents with an e are found in the sea or in electricity!)*

j) Mum used (<u>currants</u>/currents) in the Hot Cross Buns. *(Curr<u>a</u>nts are fruits – like dried gr<u>a</u>pes – currants can look like dead <u>ants</u>!)*

k) The train was (<u>stationary</u>/stationery) in the station. *(A p<u>ar</u>ked car is station<u>a</u>ry because it is not moving.)*

l) I bought my new pencil from the (stationary/<u>stationery</u>) shop *(Pap<u>er</u> and <u>e</u>nvelopes are station<u>er</u>y)*

Choose the correct word to complete the sentence. Use your dictionary to help you.

1) The man let out a loud (grown, groan)

2) The (raise, rays) of the sun were bright

3) The (hare, hair). ran across the field

4) The (hole, whole) family went on holiday

5) I wasn't sure (which, witch) was my drink.

6) The car was (stationery, stationary)

7) We paid our (fair, fare) on the bus.

8) The lion caught its (prey, pray)

9) The ball broke the (pain, pane) of glass.

10) The (current, currant) in the sea was very strong.

11) Do you like (place, plaice) and chips?

12) Do you want a (current, currant) bun?

13) What is your favourite (meat, meet)?

14) What was the (whether, weather) like while you were away?

15) She looked very (pail, pale). I was sure she was going to be ill.

16) Did you get to use your (slay, sleigh) this winter?

17) I (new, knew) that was a (new/knew) coat!

18) She (blue/blew) up the (blue/blew) balloon.

19) (Where/wear) will she (where/wear) that coat?

20) (there, they're, their) playing with (there, they're, their)

toys over (there, they're, their)

21) We should (weigh, way) them. That (weigh, way) we will know which is the heaviest.

22) People (prey, pray) in Church.

23) Is that (there/their) ball, or is it (hour/are/our) one?

<u>The Answers</u>

1) The man let out a loud (grown, <u>groan</u>)

2) The (raise, <u>rays</u>) of the sun were bright

3) The (<u>hare</u>, hair). ran across the field

4) The (hole, <u>whole</u>) family went on holiday

5) I wasn't sure (<u>which</u>, witch) was my drink.

6) The car was (stationery, <u>stationary</u>) *(A parked car is stationary – not moving)*

7) We paid our (fair, <u>fare</u>) on the bus.

8) The lion caught its (<u>prey</u>, pray) *(The prey prayed that its predator would not eat it!)*

9) The ball broke the (pain, <u>pane</u>) of glass. *(She felt a strong pain when her hand went through the pane of glass!)*

10) The (<u>current</u>, currant) in the sea was very strong.

11) Do you like (place, <u>plaice</u>) and chips?

12) Do you want a (current, <u>currant</u>) bun?

13) What is your favourite (<u>meat</u>, meet)?   *(All cats like to eat meat)*

14) What was the (whether, <u>weather</u>) like while you were away?

15) She looked very (pail, <u>pale</u>). I was sure she was going to be ill.

16) Did you get to use your (slay, <u>sleigh</u>) this winter?

17) I (new, <u>knew</u>) that was a (<u>new</u>/knew) coat!

18) She (blue/<u>blew</u>) up the (<u>blue</u>/blew) balloon.

19) (<u>Where</u>/wear) will she (where/<u>wear</u>) that coat?

20) (There, <u>they're</u>, their) playing with (there, they're, <u>their</u>)

toys over (<u>there</u>, they're, their)

21) We should (<u>weigh</u>, way) them. That (weigh, <u>way</u>) we will know which is the heaviest.

22) People (prey, <u>pray</u>) in Church.

23) Is that (there/<u>their</u>) ball, or is it (hour/are/<u>our</u>) one?

Choose the correct word from the words in the brackets

1) We were hot on the (beech, beach) as we lay in the (sun, son)

2) The colour of my jumper is (blew, blue)

3) The yacht has a (sale, sail)

4) I look in the mirror when I brush my (hare, hair)

5) It was (too, two) dark to (sea, see) at (night, knight)

6) The fruit cake had (flour, flower) and (currents, currants) in it.

7) The car was (stationery, stationary).

8) Paper and envelopes are types of (stationary, stationery)

9) A clock tells the (thyme, time) in (ours, hours) and minutes.

10) I am (too, two) (week, weak) to (peddle, pedal) my bike.

11) I (ate, eight) (plaice, place) and chips for my (tea, tee)

12) I enjoyed eating the (new, knew) (cereal, serial) for breakfast.

13) The pupils learned (to, too, two) (reed, read) and (write, right) in school.

14) The greedy child took the (hole, whole) cake rather than just a (piece, peace)

15) You are not (allowed, aloud) to (waist, waste) water in a drought.

16) (Weight, Wait) until you (here, hear) the (belle, bell) (ring, wring) before   (ewe, you) enter.

17) Is that (there, their, they're) ball or is it (our, hour, are) one

The Answers

1) We were hot on the (beech, <u>beach</u>) as we lay in the (<u>sun,</u> son)

2) The colour of my jumper is (blew, <u>blue</u>)

3) The yacht has a (sale, <u>sail</u>)

4) I look in the mirror when I brush my (hare, <u>hair</u>)

5) It was (<u>too,</u> two) dark to (sea, <u>see)</u> at (<u>night,</u> knight)

6) The fruit cake had (<u>flour,</u> flower) and (currents, <u>currants</u>) in it.

7) The car was (stationery, <u>stationary</u>).

8) Paper and envelopes are types of (stationary, <u>stationery</u>)

9) A clock tells the (thyme, <u>time</u>) in (ours, <u>hours</u>) and minutes.

10) I am (<u>too,</u> two) (week, <u>weak)</u> to (peddle, <u>pedal)</u> my bike.

11) I (<u>ate,</u> eight) (<u>plaice,</u> place) and chips for my (<u>tea,</u> tee)

12) I enjoyed eating the (<u>new,</u> knew) (<u>cereal,</u> serial) for breakfast.

13) The pupils learned (<u>to,</u> too, two) (reed, <u>read)</u> and (<u>write,</u> right) in school.

14) The greedy child took the (hole, <u>whole)</u> cake rather than just a (<u>piece,</u> peace)

15) You are not (<u>allowed</u>, aloud) to (waist, <u>waste</u>) water in a drought.

16) (Weight, <u>Wait</u>) until you (here, <u>hear</u>) the (belle, <u>bell</u>) (<u>ring</u>, wring) before   (ewe, <u>you</u>) enter.

17) Is that (there, <u>their</u>, they're) ball or is it (<u>our</u>, hour, are) one

Do you know what all the other homophones mean?

Can you use them in sentences of your own?

In each sentence, choose the word which you think is the correct one for each sentence.

1. (They're, Their) going on holiday tomorrow.

2. I (herd, heard) the wolves growling at the zoo.

3. I saw a huge (herd, heard) of cows in the field.

4. Sometimes my brother (growns, groans) if he has homework to do.

5. The child kept asking his parents (weather, whether) it was time yet.

6. In olden times, pirates used to bury their (hoard, horde) of treasure.

7. My sister heard that she had (past, passed) her exams.

8. The (pear, pair) of thieves ran when they heard the police siren.

9. On the (waist, waste) land near my house, there is a new building (site, sight)

10. The teenager was (thrown, throne) out of the cinema for being underage.

11. Yesterday, after (tea, tee), my grandfather told us some ghostly (tales, tails).

12. The old lady made sure she watched the (cereal, serial) each day.

13. We went (threw, through) a tunnel on the motorway.

14. I wasn't (shore, sure) (which, witch) path to take in the

(wood, would)

15. The girl couldn't tell if the wax model was (real, reel) or not.

16. "(Wear, Where) do you think you are going?" asked the

teacher.

The Answers

1. (They're, Their) going on holiday tomorrow.

2. I (herd, heard) the wolves growling at the zoo.

3. I saw a huge (herd, heard) of cows in the field.

4. Sometimes my brother (growns, groans) if he has homework to do.

5. The child kept asking his parents (weather, whether) it was time yet.

6. In olden times, pirates used to bury their (hoard, horde) of treasure.

7. My sister heard that she had (past, passed) her exams.

8. The (pear, pair) of thieves ran when they heard the police siren.

9. On the (waist, waste) land near my house, there is a new building (site, sight)

10. The teenager was (thrown, throne) out of the cinema for being underage.

11. Yesterday, after (tea, tee), my grandfather told us some ghostly (tales, tails).

12. The old lady made sure she watched the (cereal, serial) each day.

13. We went (threw, through) a tunnel on the motorway.

14. I wasn't (shore, <u>sure</u>) (<u>which,</u> witch) path to take in the (<u>wood,</u> would)

15. The girl couldn't tell if the wax model was (<u>real,</u> reel) or not.

16. "(Wear, <u>Where</u>) do you think you are going?" asked the teacher.

<u>Homonyms</u> are words that are usually spelt the same way, but have very different meanings. eg. a <u>wave</u> of the hand,   a <u>wave</u> at sea.

Often, they are pronounced in different ways; which makes them more complex.

Create a sentence showing an alternative meaning for each of the underlined words.

I've done the first one for you.

  a. Another word for Mum is <u>mummy.</u>

      An Egyptian mummy was found in the tomb.

  b. The <u>light</u> began to dawn.

  c. The gold was in the <u>chest</u>

  d. The petrol <u>tank</u> was empty.

  e. The doors of the <u>lift</u> opened

  f. The old lady had a walking <u>stick.</u>

  g. It is wrong to tell a <u>lie.</u>

  h. The boy <u>leaves</u> tomorrow

  i. The <u>bark</u> of the tree was rough.

  j. People keep money in a <u>bank</u>

The Answers

Many answers are feasible here; but please make sure that your child's answers show a contrasting meaning for the key word – as in the example answers that I have given.

e.g.

a. Another word for Mum is <u>mummy.</u>

An Egyptian mummy was found in the tomb.

b. The <u>light</u> began to dawn.

The package was very <u>light</u>

c. The gold was in the <u>chest</u>

I felt a sharp pain in my <u>chest</u>

d. The petrol <u>tank</u> was empty.

Soldiers might drive a <u>tank</u>

e. The doors of the <u>lift</u> opened

Can you <u>lift</u> this heavy box?

f. The old lady had a walking <u>stick.</u>

We can use glue to <u>stick</u> two pieces of paper together

g. It is wrong to tell a <u>lie.</u>

I like to <u>lie</u> in on a Sunday

h. The boy <u>leaves</u> tomorrow

The <u>leaves</u> fall off the trees in autumn.

i. The <u>bark</u> of the tree was rough.

There is a dog who lives near us who has a very piercing <u>bark</u>

j. People keep money in a <u>bank</u>

Many animals like to explore the river <u>bank.</u>

Find an alternative meaning for each of these words.

a. Date   A type of fruit

        OR

b. Ruler   A stick used for measuring

        OR

c. Swallow   Sending your food to the oesophagus

        OR

d. Bank   Where you keep your money

        OR

e. Watch   To look at something

        OR

f. Tap   Controls the flow of water

        OR

g. Wind   Moving air

        OR

h. Letter   Message received in the post

        OR

i. Ring   metal band worn on finger

        OR

j. Palm   Part of the hand

        OR

k. Trunk   An elephant's protuberance

        OR

Answers

Your child's answers may vary, but some possibilities are shown below. Make sure that your child's answers show a totally different meaning to the one shown on the previous page.

a. Date   a precise day or time

b. Ruler   A leader of a country

c. Swallow   A bird

d. Bank   The side of a river

e. Watch   Used to tell the time

f. Tap   A gentle knock e.g. on the side of the head

g. Wind   To turn a knob to provide power or movement

h. Letter   Part of the alphabet

i. Ring   To phone someone

j. Palm   A type of tree

k. Trunk   A large suitcase

Find the word that fits each of these two definitions.

a. For striking a ball   a small, winged mammal

b. Door fastener   a curl of hair

c. Something that gives light   Something you grow

d. Flesh around your teeth   a type of glue

e. Holds water   opposite of float

f. A season   to jump

g. To decline an invitation   rubbish

h. Quick, rapid   a type of bird

i. Part of your face   the top of a hill

j. A tomb   solemn or serious

k. A type of bird   to transfer food to the oesophagus.

Find the word that fits each of these two definitions.

a. Bat

b. Lock

c. Bulb

d. Gum

e. Sink

f. Spring

g. Refuse

h. Swift

i. Brow

j. Grave

k. Swallow

Try using the following homonyms in the spaces to make the sentences work. Remember, they may not be pronounced the same way both times!

Wound	leave	produce	shed	refuse	will	row	
present	desert	polish	tear	wind	sow	object	
bass	invalid	close	does	sewer	intimate	park	
minute	subject	dove					

1) The bandage was .... around the ....

2) The farm was used to ....

3) The dump was so full that it had to .... any more ....

4) We must .... the .... furniture..

5) The soldier decided to .... his camel in the ....

6) Since there is no time like the ...., he thought it was time

to .... the ....

7) A .... was painted on the head of the .... drum.

8) When shot at, the .... into the bushes.

9) I did not .... to the ....

10) The insurance was .... for the ....

11) There was a .... among the oarsmen about how to ....

12) They were too .... to the door to .... it.

13) The buck .... funny things when the .... are present.

14) A seamstress and a .... fell down into a .... pipe.

15) To help with planting, the farmer taught his .... to ....

16) The .... was too strong to .... the sail.

17) Upon seeing the ……… in the painting I shed a ……… .

18) I had to ……… the ……… to a series of tests.

19) How can I ……… this to my most ……… friend?

20) Do not ……… you car outside the ……… park gates.

20) In Autumn, the trees ……… their leaves which blow into our garden ……… .

21) The solicitor ……… draw up the ……… tomorrow.

22) The soldier had to ……… home quickly as he did not want to be absent without ……….

23) In a ………, I will show you a ……… animal, barely visible to the human eye.

The Answers

1) The bandage was <u>wound</u> around the <u>wound</u>

2) The farm was used to <u>produce produce</u>.

3) The dump was so full that it had to <u>refuse</u> any more <u>refuse</u>

4) We must <u>polish</u> the <u>Polish</u> furniture..

5) The soldier decided to <u>desert</u> his camel in the <u>desert</u>.

6) Since there is no time like the <u>present</u>, he thought it was time to <u>present</u> the present.

7) A <u>bass</u> was painted on the head of the <u>bass</u> drum.

8) When shot at, the <u>dove dove</u> into the bushes.

9) I did not <u>object</u> to the <u>object</u>.

10) The insurance was <u>invalid</u> for the <u>invalid</u> .

11) There was a <u>row</u> among the oarsmen about how to <u>row</u>.

12) They were too <u>close</u> to the door to <u>close</u> it.

13) The buck <u>does</u> funny things when the <u>does</u> are present.

14) A seamstress and a <u>sewer</u> fell down into a <u>sewer</u> line.

15) To help with planting, the farmer taught his <u>sow</u> to <u>sow</u>.

16) The <u>wind</u> was too strong to <u>wind</u> the sail.

17) Upon seeing the <u>tear</u> in the painting I shed a <u>tear</u>.

18) I had to <u>subject</u> the <u>subject</u> to a series of tests.

19) How can I <u>intimate</u> this to my most <u>intimate</u> friend?

20) Do not <u>park</u> your car outside the <u>park</u> gates.

20) In Autumn, the trees <u>shed</u> their leaves which blow into our garden <u>shed</u>.

21) The solicitor <u>will</u> draw up the <u>will</u> tomorrow.

22) The soldier had to <u>leave</u> home quickly as he did not want to be absent without <u>leave</u>.

23) In a minute, I will show you a minute animal, barely visible to the human eye.

Verb Usage

Make sure you know how to choose the correct verb form for your sentences – as this often crops up in English tests. Choose the grammatically correct option for each of these sentences.

a) Damien (is/are) best friends with Tom and Reuben

b) The Wren family (was/were) loving the theme park.

c) Why (was/were) you a little late again this morning?

d) Veejay could (saw/see) that the beans (was/were) beginning to grow.

e) Sarah (caught/catched) the ball confidently.

f) Jamie (brung/brought) the toy to school.

g) Mitchell found the homework (which/what) he had been looking for.

h) John and (me/I) went to the park at the weekend.

i) There (was/were) no moon and they couldn't see (anything/nothing) much.

j) James said that he (did/done) it himself.

k) There (was/were) time to get home before (our/are) friends arrived.

l) Marianne (is/are) comfortable in bed.

m) The dogs (was/were) chasing the rabbits.

n) "(Was/Were) you happy?" she asked.

o) There (is/are) a knock at the door.

p) Tim and Sally (is/are) friends.

The Answers

a) Damien (<u>is</u>/are) best friends with Tom and Reuben

b) The Wren family (was/<u>were</u>) loving the theme park.

c) Why (was/<u>were</u>) you a little late again this morning?

d) Veejay could (saw/<u>see</u>) that the beans (was/were) beginning to grow.

e) Sarah (<u>caught</u>/catched) the ball confidently.

f) Jamie (brung/<u>brought</u>) the toy to school.

g) Mitchell found the homework (<u>which</u>/what) he had been looking for.

h) John and (me/<u>I</u>) went to the park at the weekend.

i) There (<u>was</u>/were) no moon and they couldn't see (<u>anything</u>/nothing) much.

j) James said that he (<u>did</u>/done) it himself. *(an alternative would be <u>had done</u>)*

k) There (<u>was</u>/were) time to get home before (<u>our</u>/are) friends arrived.

l) Marianne (<u>is</u>/are) comfortable in bed.

m) The dogs (was/<u>were</u>) chasing the rabbits.

n) "(Was/<u>Were</u>) you happy?" she asked.

o) There (<u>is</u>/are) a knock at the door.

p) Tim and Sally (is/<u>are</u>) friends.

Games to Boost Your Vocabulary Skills

Post-it Note Based Games

As mentioned in the introduction, it is a good idea to write tricky words on a post-it note, along with 2 or 3 key synonyms and stick them on the toilet door, where your child will see it several times a day! (This could also lead to interesting discussions with visitors!). Encourage your child to read aloud the words on one of the post-it notes each time they go to the toilet, as this more multi-sensual approach helps the word to fix more firmly in the brain.

Turn it into a game if you can!

○ Stick a range of words in a variety of places, and see if they know which door holds the synonym for... e.g. indolent.

○ Can they add an antonym in a different colour to each post-it note?

○ Shout out three synonyms from one of the post-it notes and see if your child can add the fourth.

○ Create a Vocabulary Treasure Hunt by giving them a list of words and see if they can go around the house searching for the synonyms on the post-it notes, matching them correctly.

o Use the new words that your child is learning in games of hangman or similar.

Vocabulary Snap

This game can be adapted for children of all ages; although younger children will probably be able to give fewer synonyms. Try to use quite complex words yourself, as this is a great way to enhance your child's vocabulary.

Start off by giving a key word; preferably one that you know has quite a lot of synonyms. Can your child give a synonym for it? Take it in turns to provide additional synonyms and see how many synonyms for the key word the people in your car can provide.

At the basic level, the one who provides the last legitimate synonym wins a point; however, if you want to be more ambitious, you might like to expect the winner to provide an antonym for a bonus point.

Who will be the last to give a synonym? Will they score a point, or will one of their opponents trump them by giving a legitimate antonym?

E.g.   indolent
       Lazy
       Idle
       Slothful
       Lackadaisical
       Slack
       (Pass – I challenge you!)
       Lethargic! (1 Point)
       (Double up with an antonym!)
       DILIGENT or INDUSTRIOUS wins!!!!

The winner could then choose whether to continue the games with a series of synonyms for the antonym that they have given; or they could choose a new word altogether.

<u>Right and Left</u>

This game can be adapted for all ages from around 7 to 11 and over.

Take it in turns to give a word with a clear opposite.

The next player should try to give an antonym for that word.

If they are successful, they then give another word which the next player has to give an antonym for.

Play passes until one player gets stuck or has to repeat a word that has already been given.

e.g.

Player 1 – Large

Player 2 – tiny; sleepy

Player 3 – awake; minute

Player 4 – huge; transparent

Player 1 – opaque; stationary

Player 2 – mobile; etc.

Magic Words

This game can be played by children of all ages, although age and vocabulary strength may limit the contributions of younger players.

Each day has a new magic word – with a magic response; which could be something as simple as a star on their star chart, or which could be a treat in its own right.

Give a couple of simple clues for a 'magic word' and invite your child to ask further questions or to make a guess.

Alternatively, the person in the passenger seat could turn it into a form of hangman; particularly if you have a notebook and pencil handy.

e.g. (This is an example for a bright Year 5/6 child – particularly for one preparing for the 11+ selection tests.)

Today's Magic Word begins with L.

Can you give me a synonym?

Today's Magic Word is a synonym for you!

How many letters?

Today's Magic Word contains 10 letters

What is the third letter?

Q

Can you give me another synonym, please?

Today's Magic Word means 'chatty'. We've met it before.

LOQUACIOUS

Gimme Two (or more!) - The Homophone Game

This game can be played by children of all ages, although age and vocabulary strength may limit the contributions of younger players.

Homophones are words that sound the same as your key word BUT are spelt differently and have very different meanings. Give your child a word that has a range of homophones and see if they can put them in two or more different sentences. The spellings may be the same in some of the examples, BUT the meaning must be totally different every time.

e.g. rain (based on a question from the 2012 entry Essex English 11+ paper)

- I hate it when it rains at playtime
- Our Queen has reigned for over 60 years.
- We can use reins to control a horse.
- Rayne is a place in Essex, close to Braintree. (Believe it or not, this was accepted as an answer when they were asked to give two homophones for 'rain' in sentence format!)

e.g. current

- The strong currents pulled the boats out to sea.
- I like currants in my cakes
- What is the current news?
- Electrical currents pass the power through the circuit to light the bulb.

Who can come up with the best sentences?

Do they know the correct spellings of the homophones that they are using each time? You might like to get them to spell the word as they complete the sentence – spelling bee style.

Some other good words to include are:

Stationary/stationery   whole/hole   poor/pour/pore
grown/groan   rays/raise   hare/hair   which/witch
fair/fare   prey/pray   plaice/place   meat/meet
whether/weather   sleigh/slay   knew/new   weigh/way
there/their/they're   our/hour/are   blue/blew
flour/flower   beach/beech   sail/sale   allowed/aloud
week/weak   peace/piece   flee/flea   air/heir   scene/seen
assent/ascent   alter/altar   boy/buoy   sealing/ceiling
beach/beech   principals/principles   stare/stair   etc.

... However, there are a great many more which are easy to find on the internet!

Gimme Two More - (The Homonym Game)

This game can be played by children of all ages, although age and vocabulary strength may limit the contributions of younger players.

Whereas homophones are words which *sound* the same as the key word but are spelt, differently; homonyms are words which are *spelt* the same way, but have different meanings and, in many cases, have different sounds too.

Can your child think of more than one meaning for a key word?

Do they know more than one way to pronounce it?

Can they create a funny sentence using a pair of homonyms?

E.g. He wound the bandage around the wound.

In a minute, I will show you a minute animal that can scarcely be seen by the human eye.

Here are some key examples, but I'm sure you can find more.

Wound	leave	produce	shed	refuse	will	tear	row	
present	desert	polish	lead	wind	sow	object		
bass	invalid	close	does	sewer	intimate	park		
minute	subject	dove						

Bonus Section - A Range of Alphabet Games and Other Activities to Aid Your Child's 11+ Preparation

Games and activities relating to the alphabet and to alphabetical order are particularly good at boosting mental agility – or the speed at which we process thoughts, ideas and calculations. Good mental agility is an essential part of our processing skills, allowing us to move more rapidly from idea to idea; from concept to concept; and to calculate a range of puzzles and problems with increasing speed. As a result, they are vital tools in the preparation for the 11+

The skills in this section are designed to take your child's knowledge of the alphabet further, taking them way beyond the basics. Many of these games involved are based on activities I use regularly with 9 to 10 year olds to boost their mental agility and to help them to prepare for the 11+. Many of them can be done as simple, in car activities on the way to and from school – or whilst travelling to their grandparents. Whilst they may seem simple at first, they soon get quite a bit harder; so don't expect your child to be able to race through the ideas too quickly! Remember, little and often with regular revision is the best way to lead to mastery of a concept, helping your child to move what they've learned out of their short term memory and into the long term memory, where it will be handy for rapid work.

Where to Start?

First of all, make sure that you child is totally confident in his or her knowledge of the forwards alphabet.

This is something that we often assume, particularly once they are over 7 years old. After all, we've heard them sing the Sesame Street song and they appear to know what they are singing; however, in reality, many children struggle around the region of L, M, N, O, P, as they have got into the habit of singing them too quickly. Because M & N can sound similar, they are often reserved, causing confusion. Also, watch the last few letters, as many children get confused around the last 5 letters. See if your child can *recite* the alphabet, rather than singing it, as this will help you to ensure that they are getting the letters in the correct order.

Once you are certain that your child can confidently recite the forwards alphabet, try some of the activities over the next few pages.

Only move from one activity to the next when you are certain that they are confident with the previous stage.

Using and Developing the Forwards Alphabet

- Collect the alphabet through registration numbers.

  Starting with 'A', how many trips does it take you to complete the alphabet using the letters on the registration numbers that you see?

- Do they know which letters come 5th, 10th, 15th and 20th in the normal alphabet?

  When I am working with children, we usually refer to these as the EJOT letters; soon deciding that EJOT is an excellent insult to fire at a sibling, friend or cousin who is irritating us!

  You could use these as reward points in the previous game to help boost interest and to promote memory of these key letters.

- Using their knowledge of the EJOT letters, can they work out the position of a given letter in the alphabet?

  e.g. what's the position of the letter g in the alphabet?

- Can they tell you which letters come 13th, 19th, 8th etc. in the normal alphabet from their knowledge of EJOT?

  Who can be the first to spot the twelfth letter of the alphabet in a car's registration number?

  Look for the letter that comes 5 places after j.

  Spot the letter that comes before t in the alphabet.

In My Grandmother's Attic

This is a great game for developing memory and therefore for helping to boost mental agility.

It is a game that you have probably played many times under a great many different titles, some of which are suggested below to give seasonal or alternative twists to the theme.

Basically, you start with a statement and an item; and each player that follows has to complete the previous list and add an item of their own. It's best to work through your lists alphabetically, at least until you all become confident at the game (and certainly if you are including the driver, who needs to be able to concentrate on several things at once!)

E.g.

In my grandmother's attic, there is an antelope's head

In my grandmother's attic, there is an antelope's head and a bear skin

In my grandmother's attic, there is an antelope's head, a bear skin and a cat

In my grandmother's attic, there is an antelope's head, a bear skin, a cat and a dinosaur's egg

In my grandmother's attic, there is an antelope's head, a bear skin, a cat, a dinosaur' egg and an elephant

etc. etc.

Continue until someone makes a mistake; or until you reach the letter 'z' with perfect responses – which is extremely challenging! (It is rare to be able to pass 'm' without a lot of practice!)

Alternative Themes for similar games

In My Christmas Stocking, I found ...

When I packed my suitcase, I packed ...

When I went shopping, I bought ... (just don't ask my class what they bought – it gets quite frightening at times – particularly on the way to tennis recently!)

When I opened the fridge, I saw ... (all answers should be food items)

When I went to the zoo, I saw ... (all items should be animals)

In the market, I bought ... (items you might see at a market)

Looking out of my window, I could see ... (Like I Spy, the items viewed should be appropriate to the moment!)

When I went on holiday, I went to ... (a geographical version of the game)

My favourite cities are ...

An Alphabetical Description

This game can be played by children of all ages, although age and vocabulary strength may limit the contributions of younger players.

Can you describe yourselves or something that you are familiar with by using each letter of the alphabet in its correct order? Take it in turns to use one letter at a time, or perhaps two consecutive letters of the alphabet.

e.g. We are adorably brilliant, creatively decorative, enthusiastically ferocious, etc.

- Who can provide the best word?

- Can you think of words for x and z? You may have to think creatively for these, unless you want to be xenophobes or xenophiles! (e.g. xenophobic young zoologists!)

The more you play this game, the more likely your children are to try to think of better and increasingly unusual words that they can use – particularly if you try to introduce a few in your own turns!

If you introduce an unusual word, try to ensure that your children know what your word means; and use it regularly for a few weeks to 'fix' it in your children's vocabulary.

Thinking the Alphabet Through in a Different Way

Once your children have developed full confidence with the normal forwards alphabet, it's important that they are able to think the alphabet through in a range of different ways – not just conventionally. This will help when they have to think about and complete alphabet patterns, sort words into alphabetical order and use a conventional dictionary, thesaurus or other alphabetical reference source. As such, it is an essential lead in to the Verbal Reasoning skills that are central to the 11+ exams.

- Can they think of the alphabet like a circle and recite from one letter all the way round to that letter again.

    e.g. – Today the alphabet starts with f. Tell me the whole alphabet.

    f g h i j k l m n o p q r s t u v w x y z a b c d e
- Can they answer questions such as – if the first letter of today's alphabet is f, what is the new 6th letter? What is the penultimate letter? What is the position of the letter j? etc.

    Who can find a registration plate that contains today's 5th letter? Etc.

- Can your child recite the alphabet without any vowels? Can they work out the position of given letters using this?

    e.g. If all the vowels were removed from the alphabet, which letter would come tenth?

e.g. Who can find a registration number that contains the third vowel, or one containing the tenth consonant, or, if you want to be really challenging, one that contains both the third vowel AND the tenth consonant? Etc.

- Can they just give the alternate letters (A, C, E, G … etc.)

- Can they find pairs of alternate letters in the registration numbers they see? E.g., A & C; B & D etc.

- Play 'In My Grandmother's Attic' (or similar) starting from a different letter of the alphabet for a change. See where you end up this time!

The Backwards Alphabet

Can your child learn to recite the backwards alphabet?

This is best learnt to a rap rhythm, and divides itself nicely into groups of 3 beats (triplets), as illustrated below.

z y x, w v

u t s r q p

o n m, l k j

i h g, f e d, c b a

It can be made into a bit of a game or competition – how fast can they get? (They often want to compete with me and recite the whole thing in under 5 seconds!)

Once really learnt, it stays with you for life; just as your tables do. I remember once teaching the much younger brother of a former pupil, who had tried to earn his elder brother's sympathy by whining that he had been told to learn his backwards alphabet. Much to his chagrin, his 17 year old brother not only had no sympathy; he could also still recite the whole thing in less than 5 seconds, 7 years after having initially learnt it! Needless to say, the younger child soon learnt to do the same thing!

(Incidentally, I recently re-met the mother of both boys – some 10 years later, they can both still do it!!!)

Collect the alphabet backwards through registration numbers.

Starting with 'Z', how many trips does it take you to complete the alphabet all the way to 'A' using the letters on the registration numbers that you see?

Play 'In My Grandmother's Attic' but start with an item beginning with Z and work backwards through the alphabet towards Y

In My Grandmother's backwards Attic, there was a zebra.

In My Grandmother's Backwards Alphabet, there was a zebra and a yacht

In My Grandmother's Attic, there was a zebra, a yacht and an x ray

Etc. etc.

Alphabet Mirrors

Can your child work out the alphabet mirror pairs? These often crop up in Verbal Reasoning papers in the form of code questions as well as through letter pair codes. They are based on the idea that the centre point of the alphabet is based between the M and the N, creating a sort of 'mirror' and resulting in the pairs below.

A Z, B Y, C X, D W, E V, F U, G T, H S, I R, J Q, K P, L O, M N

- Can they invent silly phrases to help them to remember the pairs?

  e.g. alphabetical zoos, blue yachts, colourful x-rays, dead wombats etc.

  Try using those for an alternative version of 'In My Grandmother's Attic'

  e.g.   In My Alphabetical Mirror, I saw an Amber Zebra

            In My Alphabetical Mirror, I saw an Amber Zebra and a Blue Yacht

            In My Alphabetical Mirror, I saw an Amber Zebra, a Blue Yacht and   a Crushed Xylophone etc.

- Encourage them to collect the alphabet through mirror pairs. Look for registration numbers that contain one or more of the mirror pairs anywhere in the combination and keep a tally of those you have seen.

e.g. a registration number such as

Z 359 CXU

allows you to score 'CX', whereas a registration number such
as

YO 56 BLF

allows you to score both BY and OL if you are being really
observant!

How many journeys does it take you to collect the alphabet
in mirror pairs?

Excerpts from other books by the same author

These examples include only very small sections from two of my other publications. For further details, please search the actual title – where you will be able to either view the first few pages online or to download a sample free of charge and, hopefully, will be inspired to purchase or to use your Prime account to borrow the complete book!

'Can We Play Maths Today, Please?' includes a lot of ideas for games and activities, a great many of which will help any child preparing for the 11+; and the sample chapters that I have selected to go with this book all have a bearing on 11+ preparation.

- o DICE GAMES AND CARD GAMES can all be used to boost speed and accuracy in simple calculations – an essential skill when it comes to the 11+ maths papers. The Essex paper, for example, is based quite strongly on National Curriculum Level 5 and 6 questions; however, the earlier questions in the test are worth just as many marks, and are usually based on simple mathematical rules, where accuracy is integral!

- o BIDMAS is a tricky concept that frequently comes up in 11+ tests, and is something that children need to be introduced to in Years 5 & 6 if they are preparing for these exams.

'Richard's Magic Book' is a novel, written primarily for 7 to 10 year olds; although it has been enjoyed by children outside these age ranges. A small sample section has been included here.

Can We Play Maths Today, Please?

Three sample chapters which have been adapted from the book to suit trainee 11+ candidates, two of which look at activities with dice and with playing cards, plus an additional chapter introducing the concept of BIDMAS, which is essential for 11+ maths papers.

Using Dice

There are a great many games and activities that merely involve use of dice; not just board games and Yahtzee! Obviously, the more dice you use, the more complicated the games are; but the options are virtually limitless.

Two Dice

- Roll two dice and work out the product of the two numbers. Who can score the greatest total?

Three Dice

- Roll three dice and work out the sum of all three. Who can score the largest total?

- Roll two dice and work out their sum to give you your first number. Roll the third die and calculate the product of your two numbers. Who can score the greatest total? What is the highest possible total? How can you work it out?

- Roll three dice and work out the product of the three numbers rolled. Who can score the highest product? (This includes looking at cubed numbers to 6 cubed – which can be tricky, but which often occur on the maths papers)

Four Dice

- Roll four dice and work out the sum of all four. Who can score the largest total?

- Roll two dice and work out their sum to give you your first number. Next, roll the other two and work out their sum to give you your second number. Work out the product of the two numbers. Who can score the greatest total?

- Roll 4 dice; use addition and multiplication to work out the highest possible answer that can be made from your combination of numbers

- Roll all four dice. How many different totals can you make with your four dice in five minutes? Can you use some of the rules of BIDMAS (explained later) to help you?

e.g. you roll...

You could score...
1 + 2 + 3 + 4 = 10
1 x 2 x 3 x 4 = 24
(1 + 2) x (3 + 4) = 21
(1 + 2) x 3 x 4 = 36
etc.
Score 1 point for every different total made. Score 20 points to gain a 'reward'.
Year 6 children can use aspects of BIDMAS in their answers, in which case, they may like to check their answers on a scientific calculator.
<u>Six Dice</u>
- Roll all six dice and work out the total sum. Who can score the largest total?

- Roll two dice and work out their sum to give you your first number and multiply it by one of the others. Choose the three of your dice that will give the greatest product and declare it. Who can score the greatest total?

  How many different totals can your child make in 5 minutes?
- Choose 3 of your dice and work out their product. Who can score the highest product?

- Mega tricky game! Roll all six dice. How many different totals can you make with your six dice in five minutes?

e.g. you roll...

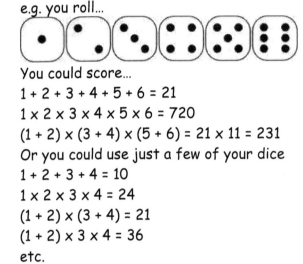

You could score...
1 + 2 + 3 + 4 + 5 + 6 = 21
1 x 2 x 3 x 4 x 5 x 6 = 720
(1 + 2) x (3 + 4) x (5 + 6) = 21 x 11 = 231
Or you could use just a few of your dice
1 + 2 + 3 + 4 = 10
1 x 2 x 3 x 4 = 24
(1 + 2) x (3 + 4) = 21
(1 + 2) x 3 x 4 = 36
etc.
Score 1 point for every different total made and 2 points for the highest total each time. Score 20 points to gain a 'reward'. 11+ candidates and Year 6 children can use aspects of BIDMAS in their answers, in which case, they may like to check their answers on a scientific calculator.

Using Polyhedral Dice

A range of different polyhedral dice can be purchased online, both through Amazon and also through eBay. Use of these widen the range of numbers usable in games and raise the limits infinitely.

Put a set of these down in front of you child from around Years 3/4 after having played a range of dice games and step back. See what they can come up with! Children can be quite ingenious with their ideas; particularly after having been challenged by use of unusual tools!

Using Playing Cards

There are literally hundreds of games that can be played using an ordinary pack of playing games. From simple number matching games such as 'snap' to games which involve more complex mathematical skills, the options are virtually limitless. Many ideas have been included in the year group sections of this book; however, here are a few others that you might like to try.

Snap

Everyone knows this game! Divide the cards equally between the players; then take it in turns to place a card on the pile. When the two top cards match, the first player to shout 'snap' takes the pile. The winner is the player with the most cards at the end of game.

Thirteen

Like 'snap' but this time you shout when the top two cards total 13. In this game, an ace counts as 1, jack as 11, queen as 12 and king as 13 (so wins as a solo card!)

Twenty Four

As above, but this time looking at the product of the top two cards. When the product is 24, shout out!

Because 24 is a number that has a lot of factors, it is a fairly easy total to work towards; however, you might like to change the challenge to other numbers. Any multiple of 12 is good – 36 is very good!

Deal 'em - Adders.

This activity is great for rapid addition work and number bond revision.

Remove all the 'royal' cards from the pack, leaving you with a standard pack of ace to ten cards in the four suits. Shuffle the cards thoroughly and place them face down on the table. Take it in turns to turn over the top card, adding its total to the ones already turned.

e.g. You turn over the 5

Your child turns over the 7 and shouts out '12'
You turn over a 6 – your child shouts '18'
Your child turns over a 3 – '21' etc.

Deal 'em – Subtractors.
Play as above, but subtract from 110
e.g. You turn over the 5. Your child shouts out '105'
Your child turns over the 7 and shouts out '98'
You turn over a 6 – your child shouts '92'
Your child turns over a 3 – '89' etc.

Deal 'em Positive and negative
This is a game for children from the top of Year 4 into years 5 and 6
Just like the previous games, remove the 'royal' cards from your hand first, then shuffle the cards and place them in a pile in the centre of the table. Turn them over, one at a time. In this version of the game, however, black cards are 'positive' – so you add those. Red cards are negative – so their scores are subtracted from the total.
If played correctly, your final total should be 0; although you should pass through a range of negative numbers in the process. Once your child gets good at this, you might like to 'fiddle' the shuffle to ensure that 3 or 4 red cards are encountered in a row, ensuring the use if negative totals – if you think you can get away with a bit of simple cheating!

Jubilee
A game for between 2 & 8 players (although for more than 4 players, I recommend the use of 2 packs of cards).
Starting with a full set of cards, shuffle them carefully and place them in the centre of the table.

One player turns over the cards, mentally adding each number to the previous total until a Royal card (Jack, Queen or King) is turned – at which point, the opponents shout 'Jubilee'. Their score is frozen and written down before the turn is passed to the next player.

If they get another go, they continue from their previous total. The winner is the one who has reached the highest total once the last card has been turned.

Variations on this Game

Whilst at the earlier stages, you might like to shout 'Jubilee' for every Royal card; once your child becomes more confident, you may want to save this purely for Kings.

Jubilee Plus & Jubilee Minus.

Starting with a full set of cards, shuffle them carefully and place them in the centre of the table.

In this version of the game, red cards are all negative; whereas black cards are always positive.

One player turns over the cards, adding or subtracting each number to/from the previous total until a Royal card is turned – at which point, the opponents shout 'Jubilee'. Their score is frozen and written down before the turn is passed to the next player.

If they get another go, they continue from their previous total. The winner is the one who has reached the highest total once the last card has been turned.

Variation on this Game

Whilst at the earlier stages, you might like to shout 'Jubilee' for every Royal card; once your child becomes more confident, you may want to save this purely for Kings, which results in speedier play.

Deal 'em Tables.

Take a pack of cards and remove all the 'Royals'. Shuffle well and place upside down on the table. Take it in turns to turn over the top card and multiply it to the one previously on top, calling out the product of the two.

e.g. You turn over the 5

Your child turns over a 7 and calls out ' 5 x 7 = 35'

You turn over a 4 – '7 x 4 = 28'

Your child turns over an 8 – '4 x 8 = 32'

You turn over a 6 – '6 x 8 = 48'

Etc.

If your child is good at this, introduce the 'Royals' so that a jack is 11, a Queen is 12 and a King is 13; then play as above.

To make it really hard, try making the red cards negative numbers and the black cards positive. What do they do when they turn 2 red cards over? What happens with a red card and a black one? Is it always the same?

Twenty-one

This is a simplified version of the casino game, without the gambling involved. Deal 2 cards to your child and two to yourself. They look at their cards and add up the total, deciding whether any Ace in their hand counts as a 1 or 11. All other 'royal' cards count as 10. They then decide whether to stick (keep their current total) or twist (risk taking another card). You then turn your cards over. The player whose total is nearest to, but not exceeding, 21 is the winner and scores a point. Anyone who has scored exactly 21 scores 2 points. Score 3 points if you have manages it in 2 cards. Set a target number of points for the end of the match and stick to it.

Regal Twenty-one

Make '21' more complex by counting the 'Royal' cards as: jack = 11; Queen = 12; King = 13. Score as above.

BIDMAS

As you will have noticed from the sections above, by Years 5 & 6, your child will be moving on to some quite difficult aspects of maths; one of the trickiest of which is BIDMAS (sometimes also referred to as BODMAS). This is a concept that often catches parents out, as well as children. Frequently, I have parents ask me why the answer to a question is wrong, and then I find myself having to explain BIDMAS to them as well!

Here is a brief explanation of what BIDMAS is all about for those of you who are unsure.

First of all, however, try this sum

$$4 + 6 \times 8 =$$

If you said 52; well done! You clearly already know what BIDMAS is. If, however, your response was 80 and you can't see where I got my answer of 52 from; don't worry. You are not alone, but you will need to read the explanation below!

This type of problem catches a lot of people out, and a normal calculator will also give you the faulty answer of 80 for this particular question. The reason is that it is incapable of sorting the whole sum and so dealing the relative parts of the problem in the correct order. If you try the same sum on a scientific calculator, you will see that it believes that the answer should be 52, because it doesn't solve the problem as you input each section and so is able to apply the rules of BIDMAS; which state the order of any calculation should be:

- Brackets – these should always be solved first, wherever they might appear in the sum

- Indices or Powers Of – e.g. 5^2. These should be solved next, regardless of where they appear in the sum.

- Division & Multiplication. These are solved next; but this time, they are solved in the order that they appear in the sum.

- Addition & Subtraction. When only addition and subtraction are left, start from the left hand side and work through them in the order in which they appear in the sum.

In other words, you should always multiply BEFORE adding; even if the addition looks to come first in the sum.
6 x 8 = 48 + 4 = 52. (An answer of 80 is usually described as being a BADMIS in my class, for more reasons than one!)

Example 2
What is 4 + 5 x 3?
In BIDMAS, multiplication comes before addition, so multiply 5 by 3 first.

4 + 5 x 3 = 4 + 15 = 19, so this is the right answer.

(27 is a BADMIS – you have added before multiplying.)

If you think you are beginning to understand this tricky concept, have a go at the examples overleaf; then look at my answers and explanations on the following page.

Check your understanding here!

Using BIDMAS, can you work out the value of the following?

(Answers and explanations are on the next page.)

a) 4 × 5 - 3 × 2

b) (2 + 3) × (5 - 1)

c) 2 + 6 ÷ 2

d) 8 - (6 - 1)

e) 3 × (4 + 2)

f) 4 + 5 × 12 - 7^2

g) (4 + 5) × 12 - 7^2

h) 6 – 1 x 0 + 2 ÷ 2 =

(This particular sum has been circulating on Facebook and on the internet quite a lot recently – with the claim that only 50% of people can get it right!)

Answers and explanation:

a) 4 x 5 + 3 x 2 = 14.

   In BIDMAS, multiplication comes before subtraction, so you should work out the multiplication first and then do the subtraction in order to get the correct answer:
   4 × 5 - 3 × 2 = 20 - 6 = 14

b) (2 + 3) x (5 – 1) = 20
   Solve the brackets first, so that the working is

   (2 + 3) = 5; (5 - 1) = 4; 5 × 4 = 20

c) 2 + 6 ÷ 2 = 5

   In BIDMAS division comes before addition, so

   2 + 6 ÷ 2 = 2 + 3 = 5

d) 8 – (6 – 1) = 3

   Brackets come first, so

   8 - (6 - 1) = 8 - 5 = 3

e) 3 x (4 + 2) = 18

   BIDMAS states that brackets come before multiplication, so work out the bracket first:

   (4 + 2) = 6, so

   3 × (4 + 2) = 3 × 6 = 18

f) 4 + 5 x 12 - 7^2 = 15
   First come the indices. 7^2 **is 49.**

   Next comes the multiplication. **5 × 12 = 60**

   You now have the sum **4 + 60 – 49**

4 + 60 = 64. 64 – 49 = 15

g) (4 + 5) x 12 – 7² = 59

> Brackets come first. **4 + 5 = 9**
> Indices come next. **7² = 49**
> This is followed by the multiplication. **9 x 12 = 108**
> Finally, you can tackle the subtraction.
> **108 – 49 = 59**

h) 6 – 1 x 0 + 2 ÷ 2 = 7

> Multiply first (1 x 0 = 0)
> Divide next (2 ÷ 2 – 1)
> This leaves you with the sum 6 – 0 + 1 = 7

Activities Relating to BIDMAS
Scientific Calculator Play
Children enjoy playing with calculators; particularly as it enables them to tackle problems with much bigger numbers that they would normally dream of trying. Up until know, your child will predominantly have been using a normal calculator; however, by Year 6, your child should be beginning to explore the more complex Scientific Calculators that they will be using in Senior school (However, they are better to use a normal calculator for their SATs tests, as the scientific ones tend to be a bit too complicated for the requirements of these tests and can result in very confused answers)
Give your child a scientific calculator and let them explore it first; then try setting some challenges – what sums can they make?

Challenge them to type in 7 x 6 + 4. Next, get them to try 6 + 4 x 7. Do they expect the answers to be the same? Why not? What happens? Would this happen on a normal calculator? Which part of the calculation has their calculator done first? Why?

Get them to try a few more questions like this and to see what they notice? This is a great introduction to the rules of BIDMAS!

Other BIDMAS activities
You will need an ordinary calculator and a scientific calculator for this activity. You will also need a set of digit cards from 0 to 9 in order to randomly generate target numbers.

Ask a question such as 'what is 6 + 4 x 5?' See what your child's instinctive reaction is, and then get them to try it on both calculators. Look at how the answers vary. Can your child see what the scientific calculator is doing?

Try a few more similar questions e.g.

- 5 + 3 x 8

- 3 + 12 x 3

- 6 + 8 x 5 – 7

- 7 – 4 x 6 (particularly interesting, as it takes us into negative numbers on the Scientific Calculator)

Once your child has begun to grasp the idea of BIDMAS, use a set of digit cards to randomly generate a 2 digit number. Compete with your child to create a BIDMAS sum that gives the correct answer. The most complex sum which the scientific calculator agrees with scores a point – the first player to score 10 points wins!

To find well over a hundred more ideas of mathematical games and activities to play with your child – from general games and activities suitable for children of most ages to carefully differentiated ideas for every year group from Reception to Year 6, go to www.amazon.co.uk and download 'Can We Play Maths Today, Please'

http://www.amazon.co.uk/Play-Maths-Today-Please-ebook/dp/B0085P7UKU/ref=pd_sim_sbs_kinc_1

Richard's Magic Book – Opening Chapter

Chapter 1   Why Me?

Richard was eight and a half years old and, like a lot of other boys and girls of his age, he just wasn't interested in reading. It wasn't that he couldn't read. In fact, he could read quite well when he wanted to. The main problem was that there were so many more interesting things that he could have been doing:- playing football, watching television, building things with his Lego set, playing on the computer or with his Gameboy, or just playing with his friends. In fact, almost anything was preferable to reading. Reading just got in the way; and some of the books were so dull! Nothing much happened in them, and when it did, it was so unbelievable! They were always about children with funny names - Biff, Chip and Kipper for example, or Roger Red-Hat and Billy Blue-Hat. They were never about children with nice, normal names like his own; until, that is, the day his teacher handed him a brand new book.

"I got this especially for you, Richard," Mr James had said as he gave it to him. "As soon as I saw the title, I thought of you. I just had to get it; it had your name on it!"   And when Richard looked at the title, he realised that his teacher was right. It DID have his name on it - in big letters, all over the front cover!

Richard's
Magic Book

by N. C. Lever-Clogs

"You might find it a bit hard to start with," Mr James had
added, "but keep going and I'm sure you'll find it's worth it!" He
winked at Richard. "It's a special one!"

"Thanks, Sir," Richard had replied - but he hadn't really meant
it. This book was much thicker than the ones he normally picked
up - over 60 pages - and it had <u>chapters!</u> Oh no! At 5 or 6
pages a day (his normal rate) it would take him **forever** to read!
"Oh crumbs!" he thought to himself. "It's not fair! Why couldn't
it have Amy's name on it - or Peter's? At least they liked
reading! Why couldn't it have anyone else's name but mine?" He
shoved it into the bottom of his backpack, ready to take home.
"I bet it's really dull as well!" he muttered under his breath.
"Books always are!"

It wasn't until much later that night that Richard began to realise that this book might actually be rather different from anything he had ever read before. Just before bedtime, his mother called to him to come and read, and so reluctantly, he opened it and began reading the first few sentences slowly and carefully to his mother.

Chapter 1

Richard was like a lot of other boys and girls of his age. He just wasn't interested in reading. It wasn't that he couldn't read (although it was sometimes a bit hard to put the letters together to make a proper word!)
The main problem was that there were so many more interesting things that he could have been doing:- playing football, watching television, building things with his Lego set, playing with his computer or his Gameboy, even playing with his friends, anything! Reading just got in the way, and some of the books were so dull! Nothing much happened in them, and when it did, it was so unbelievable!
They were always about children with funny names - Biff, Chip and Kipper for example, or Roger Red-Hat and Billy Blue-Hat. They were never about children with nice, normal names like his own.

"Hey!" Richard said to his Mum, "This book really could be about me! That's how I feel every night!"
"It certainly could!" his mother replied. She was fed up with all the battles to try and get Richard to read a few pages of his book each night, and was longing for him to begin to want to

read for himself. Slowly and carefully they continued reading the next two pages together, then he turned over again and was astounded to see that he had read the first chapter already. It had been a lot shorter than he had feared!

"You see, Richard! You can do it!" his mother said, happily. "It's not that hard really!"

"I suppose not," Richard replied, as he put his book back into his book bag and went upstairs to bed. He was still thinking about what he had just read. The child in the book seemed to be so much like him, it was amazing! "I wonder......." he thought to himself. "But no - it couldn't possibly be......"

Is Richard's book really magic? Is it really reading his mind, and what will it be able to do?

To find out more, go to www.amazon.co.uk and download Richard's Magic Book.

http://www.amazon.co.uk/Richards-Magic-Book-
ebook/dp/B0054GLVYY/ref=sr_1_1?s=digital-
text&ie=UTF8&qid=1365983388&sr=1-
1&keywords=Richard%27s+Magic+Book

Printed in Great Britain
by Amazon